A Moving Image of Eternity

Timaeus and Creation

Richard E. Ford

iUniverse

A MOVING IMAGE OF ETERNITY
TIMAEUS AND CREATION

iUniverse books may be ordered through booksellers or by contacting:

iUniverse
1663 Liberty Drive
Bloomington, IN 47403
www.iuniverse.com
844-349-9409

Because of the dynamic nature of the Internet, any web addresses or links contained in this book may have changed since publication and may no longer be valid. The views expressed in this work are solely those of the author and do not necessarily reflect the views of the publisher, and the publisher hereby disclaims any responsibility for them.

Any people depicted in stock imagery provided by Getty Images are models,
and such images are being used for illustrative purposes only.
Certain stock imagery © Getty Images.

ISBN: 978-1-6632-3241-0 (sc)
ISBN: 978-1-6632-3242-7 (e)

Library of Congress Control Number: 2021923962

Print information available on the last page.

iUniverse rev. date: 03/03/2022

All men, Socrates, who have any degree of right feeling, at the beginning of every enterprise, whether small or great, always call upon God.
—Timaeus

Dedicated to Plato, without whose wisdom and understanding of science the keys to the ages may have been lost forever.

Contents

Acknowledgments

The image on the front cover was created by Mandy Fonatana and was made available through Pixabay, an online graphics and photographs provider, under the terms of its license for commercial use.

About the Author

Richard Ford is a graduate of the US Coast Guard Academy and a career coast guard officer. Among his experiences was becoming adept at celestial navigation, a time-honored practical application of astronomy.

He has studied ancient architecture extensively for many years and has identified a number of mathematical concepts and geometrical shapes that reflect a much larger cosmic order, and he came to understand the importance of patterns in the cosmos.

Over the years, as many before him did, he developed a fascination with Plato's *Timaeus* that grew with time until its relationship to the cosmic patterns gradually dawned on him. Much of what he had learned over several decades was also present in *Timaeus*, and he decided it was so important that he determined to interpret the mathematical and geometric portions of the *Timaeus* text. As its detail began to emerge, he realized that not only was this work directly related to his own earlier efforts, but it also underlay all of it, and as Timaeus states, it is the foundational basis for all creation.

Introduction

Of all Plato's dialogues, the *Timaeus*, more simply Timaeus, is among the most challenging to read and comprehend, and it is fraught with unique challenges because of its frequent reference to number and geometry. Ostensibly, it was written some 2,350 years ago, around 360 BC. Benjamin Jowett (1817–1893), one of the better-known translators of Timaeus, stated, "Of all the writings of Plato, the Timaeus is the most obscure and repulsive to the modern reader."[1] Regardless, it was also an invaluable and frequently cited reference work for early astronomers and particularly Johannes Kepler (1571–1630), who used Timaeus's mathematics and geometry in their work. However, even they seemed incapable of a thorough and complete understanding of it.

In any case, Timaeus is not a text that can be easily read and comprehended. It requires careful reading, deep, purposeful reflection, and a thorough understanding of mathematics and geometry, but it is an extremely rewarding effort. Of all the texts in history that delve into the nature of God, the origins of the universe, and the fundamentals of creation, it is the most detailed and comprehensive and in many ways the most beautiful. In every respect, it is a masterpiece for the ages, an enduring, priceless treasure.[2]

Many since Plato have written about Timaeus, and doubtless many will continue to do so. I am certain that each of their works was well researched and well presented, but I will not catalogue or reference their works in mine because I have focused on the number and geometry in it to the exclusion of much else. For me, the number and geometry are not a reflection of an early yet incomplete scientific understanding of the physical universe they describe. Rather, they are a succinct and perfectly accurate reflection of an underlying and unifying principle found in these numbers and their associated geometry.

In the words of Timaeus, this principle is the "image of eternity" on which the universe was created, an image "*moving according to number* while eternity rests in unity" [37] (Note: For

---

[1] Wikipedia "Timaeus (dialogue)" Timaeus (dialogue) - Wikipedia Accessed November 11, 2021. See final section, headed, **Later influence**, the final sentence.

[2] I cite and reference Jowett's translation of Timaeus throughout this book. A copy of the Jowett version from beginning to Stephanus [57] is in appendix 1. It was downloaded and copied courtesy of the Internet Classics Archive and is available online at http://classics.mit.edu/Plato/timaeus.html However, note that the online version does <u>not</u> have Stephanus numbers, while the copy included as appendix 1, does.

numbers in brackets, see 'Stephanus numbers' mentioned below.) (emphasis added), in other words, an image created and based on the perfection of God but moving in time thus not sharing in the eternal nature of its creator but mortal. This image is the pattern "intelligible and always the same" while the visible universe is "only the imitation of the pattern, generated and visible" [49]. The pattern is perfect while the visible universe is not.

I will attempt to describe this pattern in as much detail as possible, but the scientific measure of and understanding of the visible universe with all its particulars are as accurate as humanly possible. I have no issue or dispute with any of these measures or the broad understanding of their physical reality. However, they are the imperfect, visible reality that is reflective of an underlying pattern, which is perfect. How then to resolve this seemingly irreconcilable contradiction? Perhaps the simplest way is to understand that while God's plan or pattern for creation is perfect, Mother Nature's execution of it is measurably less so. It is broadly speaking the difference between construction plans for a project and the completed project, which ends up in an acceptable range of deviation.

This is not to disparage Mother Nature or her demonstrated abilities; she is a superb craftsman and has adhered to the divine plan as closely as possible. However, fitting ideal parts together in a moving image of eternity so that the parts all retain their ideal dimensions was an almost insurmountable task, but the result was as close to the plan as possible. Almost all the parts had to be trimmed, stretched, etc. to make everything work.

It also needs to be understood that the pattern uses root numbers and the various species of these root numbers. The number 3, for example, can be understood as 300,000, 30, .003, or .00003, all of which have the same root number, 3. Similarly, $\sqrt{3}$, $\sqrt[3]{3}$, 3^2, 3^3, and 1/3 are all species of 3. In each of these examples, the number 3 is readily discernable. Broadly speaking, the pattern arises from the numbers 2 and 3, their species, and their geometric progression, i.e., 2, 4, 8, 16 etc. and 3, 9, 27, 81 etc. Also, the golden ratio, 1.61803, factors in the pattern. All of this is spoken to directly in Timaeus. The pattern will be explained in detail in the main body of the text.

The interconnectedness—or harmony as Timaeus describes it—of the pattern is one of its distinguishing features. It relates measures of distance to measures of time, and it is perfect in every sense.

For reference purposes to the text of Timaeus, the relevant section(s) are cited by their Stephanus numbers. These numbers are imbedded in the text using brackets such as [23] or [56], and they allow cited sections of the text to be located in the main body. However, only that portion of the text relevant to this work is reproduced here: [17]–[56]. Appropriate passages of Timaeus are quoted extensively in each chapter where necessary while the entire relevant text from Timaeus is in appendix 1. Using the embedded Stephanus numbers, it is fairly easy to cross-reference the quoted passages with that text.

Throughout this work, there are frequent references to Wikipedia articles for source and background. This is done only in those instances where the material is of a noncontroversial nature and where the references cited in Wikipedia are extensive and authoritative. The use of Wikipedia is done for convenience and because much of the material in this work crosses many scientific disciplines, a situation where an encyclopedia such as Wikipedia is an ideal reference provided it is well sourced.

For the general reader and those not comfortable with mathematics including number and geometry, this will be a difficult text to navigate and comprehend, but it will be an extremely profitable read for patient and persistent readers.

CHAPTER 1

The Triangles of Timaeus and Their Relationship to Number and Measure

There are two triangles from which God organized and fashioned the material universe with the four elements: earth, wind, fire, and water. The relevant text in Timaeus is found at Stephanus numbers [53]–[56] and is quoted below.

> In the first place, then, as is evident to all, fire and earth and water and air are bodies. And every sort of body possesses solidity, and every solid must necessarily be contained in planes; and every plane rectilinear figure is composed of triangles; and all triangles are originally of two kinds, both of which are made up of one right and two acute angles; one of them has at either end of the base the half of a divided right angle, having equal sides, while in the other the right angle is divided into unequal parts, having unequal sides. These, then, proceeding by a combination of probability with demonstration, we assume to be the original elements of fire and the other bodies; but the principles which are prior to these God only knows, and he of men who is the friend God. And next we have to determine what are the four most beautiful bodies which are unlike one another, and of which some are capable of resolution into one another; for having discovered thus much, we shall know the true origin of earth and fire and of the proportionate and intermediate elements. And then we shall not be willing to allow that there are any distinct kinds of visible bodies fairer than these. Wherefore we must endeavour to construct the four forms of bodies which excel in beauty, and then we shall be able to say that we have sufficiently apprehended their nature. [54] Now of the two triangles, the isosceles has one form only; the scalene or unequal-sided has an infinite number. Of the infinite forms we must select the most beautiful, if we are to proceed in due order, and any one who can

1

point out a more beautiful form than ours for the construction of these bodies, shall carry off the palm, not as an enemy, but as a friend. Now, the one which we maintain to be the most beautiful of all the many triangles (and we need not speak of the others) is that of which the double forms a third triangle which is equilateral; the reason of this would be long to tell; he who disproves what we are saying, and shows that we are mistaken, may claim a friendly victory. Then let us choose two triangles, out of which fire and the other elements have been constructed, one isosceles, the other having the square of the longer side equal to three times the square of the lesser side.

Now is the time to explain what was before obscurely said: there was an error in imagining that all the four elements might be generated by and into one another; this, I say, was an erroneous supposition, for there are generated from the triangles which we have selected four kinds—three from the one which has the sides unequal; the fourth alone is framed out of the isosceles triangle. Hence they cannot all be resolved into one another, a great number of small bodies being combined into a few large ones, or the converse. But three of them can be thus resolved and compounded, for they all spring from one, and when the greater bodies are broken up, many small bodies will spring up out of them and take their own proper figures; or, again, when many small bodies are dissolved into their triangles, if they become one, they will form one large mass of another kind. So much for their passage into one another. I have now to speak of their several kinds, and show out of what combinations of numbers each of them was formed. The first will be the simplest and smallest construction, and its element is that triangle which has its hypotenuse twice the lesser side. When two such triangles are joined at the diagonal, and this is repeated three times, and the triangles rest their diagonals and shorter sides on the same point as a centre, a single equilateral triangle is formed out of six triangles; and four equilateral triangles, if put together, make out of every three plane angles one solid angle, being that which is nearest to the most obtuse of plane angles; [55] and out of the combination of these four angles arises the first solid form which distributes into equal and similar parts the whole circle in which it is inscribed. The second species of solid is formed out of the same triangles, which unite as eight equilateral triangles and form one solid angle out of four plane angles, and out of six such angles the second body is completed. And the third body is made up of 120 triangular elements, forming twelve solid angles, each of them included in five plane equilateral triangles, having altogether twenty bases, each of which is an equilateral triangle. The one element [that is, the triangle which has its hypotenuse twice the lesser side] having generated these figures, generated no more; but the isosceles triangle produced the fourth elementary figure, which is compounded of four such triangles, joining their right angles in a centre, and forming one equilateral quadrangle. Six of these united form eight solid angles, each of which is made by the combination of three plane right angles; the figure of the body thus composed is a cube, having six plane quadrangular equilateral bases. *There was yet a fifth combination which God used in the delineation of the universe.* (emphasis added)

The two triangles chosen are depicted below.

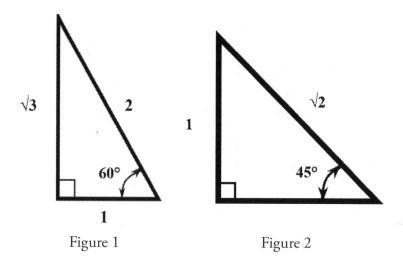

Figure 1   Figure 2

Figure 1 depicts a 30°–60°–90° triangle, the first of two triangles; figure 2 depicts the second triangle, an isosceles triangle with angles 45°–90°–45°.

These two triangles were used to create the four solids (widely referred to as the Platonic solids) described in Timaeus. The first three solids are composed of the first triangle while the fourth is composed of the second. The most complex solid is the third, which is widely referred to as the icosahedron[3] (figure 3, below). While the icosahedron is composed of 120 triangles of the first kind, it is comprehended as two succinct geometric figures: the equilateral triangle and the pentagon.

Another figure in the internal structures of the icosahedron, the golden rectangle, expands outward from a square. (The internal structures of the icosahedron are discussed in more detail

---

[3] Wikipedia, "Regular Icosahedron,", https://en.wikipedia.org/wiki/Regular_icosahedron accessed February 16, 2021. Note the drawing at the beginning, which can be animated. Drawing 3 is from table at "Uniform colorings and sub symmetries."

and a figure is provided in chapter 12.) Of note, the pentagon and the golden rectangle are related to the golden ratio. The pentagon incorporates the five-pointed star each line of which intersects with another to form the golden ratio. The golden rectangle expands out from the original square to create an endless progression of golden rectangles all of which incorporate the golden ratio in their dimensions.

It is noteworthy that since the golden rectangle derives from a square, the icosahedron also incorporates the second triangle's √2 factor found at its diagonal (see figure 2).

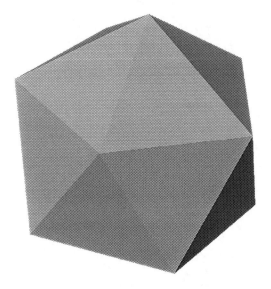

Figure 3
Regular icosahedron[4]

a. The Irrational Numbers Generated from the Icosahedron and Their Significance

The icosahedron thus incorporates three irrational, or nonwhole, numbers: √3 or 1.7320508, √2 or 1.4142135, and the golden ratio or 1.61803. When multiplied together, these three numbers yield 3.9633576589. If they are instead multiplied by 10 (permitted when using root numbers as described in the introduction), we obtain

17.320508075
14.142135623
16.180339887

Multiplying these three numbers together (17.320508075 · 14.143135623 · 16.180339887) yields 3,963.3576589, which is extremely close to the most modern calculation of Earth's equatorial

[4] Drawing credit: Tomruen, "Uniform Polyhedron–53-t2png," https://commons.wikimedia.org/wiki/File:Uniform_polyhedron-53-t2.png, in gray scale, accessed February 16, 2021.

radius in international (SI System of Measures) or statute miles: 3963.190608.[5] The equatorial circumference of the Earth in miles using the irregular numbers derived from the icosahedron is 24,902.5 miles, while the World Geodetic Survey (WGS)-84 equivalent measure from the reference ellipsoid is 24,901.461 miles, a miniscule difference of approximately one mile.[6] So Earth's equatorial circumference based on Timaeus is 24,902.5 miles.

This might be attributable to pure coincidence, but Timaeus concludes this section by stating, "There was yet a fifth combination which God used in the delineation of the universe." Most scholars believe that this statement is to be understood as a reference to a fifth Platonic solid, composed of pentagons, but it is not mentioned in Timaeus's text. The language of this statement clearly states that there was "yet a *fifth combination*" (emphasis added), not a fifth solid. The only logical interpretation then is that it is a specific reference to a fifth combination of the original two triangles, which is exactly what is found in the icosahedron, as described earlier.

This measure in miles is quite surprising given that the measure of the mile is widely believed to have originated in and been established in English law in the sixteenth century during the reign of Queen Elizabeth I and called the statute mile. But this cannot be! It must be a coincidence although seemingly a rather remarkable one. In fact, as will be shown, it is one of the most fundamental measures of the universe.

However, if readers are convinced that mere coincidence is at play here, perhaps several more apparent coincidences will cause them to reconsider. (I will of necessity anticipate here what I will be describing in far more detail in the next chapter.) In the measure of daily time, there are

- 86,400 seconds (1,440 minutes · 60 seconds/minute) in a whole day,
- 43,200 seconds in half a day, and
- 21,600 seconds in a quarter of a day.

Again, using these numbers as root numbers—864, 432, and 216 respectively—these numbers correspond to several noteworthy linear measures as follows.

864,000 (compare w. diameter of the Sun: 864,377 miles[7])
4,320 (compare w. diameter of Earth's core: 4,325 miles[8])

---

[5] Wikipedia, "Mile," https://en.wikipedia.org/wiki/Mile#:~:text=The%20mile%20is%20an%20English%20unit%20of%20length,exactly%201,609.344%20metres%20by%20international%2 accessed February 19, 2021.

[6] Wikipedia, "Earth's Radius," https://en.wikipedia.org/wiki/Earth_radius accessed February 19, 2021. This is a good, well-sourced discussion of the various measures of earth's dimensions.

[7] Wikipedia, "List of Solar System objects by size," https://en.wikipedia.org/wiki/List_of_Solar_System_objects_by_size, accessed February 19, 2021.

[8] Wikipedia, "Structure of Earth," https://en.wikipedia.org/wiki/List_of_Solar_System_objects_by_size accessed November 11, 2021. Cited value derives from the table of values.

2,160 (compare w. diameter of the Moon: 2,159.365 miles[9])

Interesting, but probably just another oddity, right? We'll derive one more number, one of the most important measures in science, using the original number generated from the three irrational numbers that derive from the icosahedron: 3.9633576589, the number obtained by multiplying 1.7320508075 ($\sqrt{3}$) · 1.41421356123 ($\sqrt{2}$) · 1.6180339887. When squared, this number divided by 10 and multiplied by 2 equals 3.14164079, which compares to the actual measure of pi (π) 3.141592653, a remarkable difference of a mere .0000481329. Timaeus's derived measure for π is likely accurate enough for most modern applications.

The measure of pi or π based on Timaeus is 3.14164079. We are likely beyond any possibility that mere coincidence is at work here. It should also be noted that pi is related to phi, as pi/4 = 0.7853981 and $\sqrt{1}$/phi = 0.7861514.

b. Important Measures Generated from Earth's Circumference

Timaeus notes a number of times in his narrative that the circle is fundamental to creation both as a physical shape and as a motion with time itself being a circular motion. The accurate measure of pi, then, permits the precise measure of the circle in all its manifestations. Furthermore, never forget that pi derives from the golden ratio and the two triangles, which according to Timaeus underly the dimensions of the created universe.

There are three more numbers that can be derived from the three irrational numbers and the circumference of Earth (24,902 miles) where the three irrational numbers were each multiplied by a factor of 10. These numbers then are

- 17.320508075
- 14.142135623
- 16.180339887

Dividing each of these numbers in turn into Earth's circumference results in the following.

- 24,902 miles/17.320508075 yields 1,437.7176, approx. equal ($\approx$) to 1,440 mins/day
- 24,902 miles/14.142135623 yields 1,760.8370 $\approx$ 1760 yds/mile
- 24,902 miles/16.180339887 yields 1,539.0282 $\approx$ 1,540 (See discussion following.)

The significance of these three numbers is that they all relate to fundamental Earth measures. In the case of the 1,437.7176 (derived from 17.320508075), this number is approximately equal

---

[9] Wikipedia, "List of Solar System objects by size," https://en.wikipedia.org/wiki/List_of_Solar_System_objects_by_size accessed November 11, 2021

to the number of minutes in a day, 1,440. However, there is a closer match between the derived number, 1,437.7176, with the number of sidereal minutes in a day, 1,436.65.

In the case of 1,760.873 (derived from 14.142135623), this number is approximately equal to the number of yards in a mile, 1,760. From this measure, the international foot or statute foot of 304.8mm is derived, and virtually all measures of volume and weight derive from the foot. (This is an outsized claim but one for which I will offer further evidence in a later chapter. But suffice to say for the moment that it is directly related to ancient Egyptian measures.)

In the case of 1,539.0282, this number is approximately equal to 1,540, a number that when cubed and divided by $(10)^7$ equals 365.2264, a number that is a remarkably close to the length of the tropical year, which is also referred to as the solar year. The tropical year is the length of time it takes for the Sun to complete its apparent return to its prior position with respect to Earth's seasons, vernal equinox to vernal equinox, 365.2417 days.

With these three measures, we are again confronted with numbers that are close approximations of their actual counterparts, but in each instance, there is a difference. However, as was explained earlier, these three numbers represent a plan or design from which reality differs. The number that has the largest error is 1,437.7176 when compared with the actual measure of 1,440 minutes/day, but this is a measure that can be readily adapted to a broader system of measures to make it compatible. But who made the adaption? Good question, though it is one best deferred for the moment.

There is one more number that can be produced from the two triangles and the golden ratio: the speed of light. The beginning of this calculation is: $(\sqrt{phi} \cdot \sqrt{2}) \div \sqrt{3}$, or (1.27201964 1.4142135) ÷ 1.7320508) = 1.0386. Next, multiply 1.0386 · 2 = 2.0772. Next, multiply $(2.0772)^4$ = 18.61715247. And finally multiply 18.61715247 · 10,000 = 186,171 miles/second, which compares with the modern figure of 186,282 miles/second, a difference of 110.5 miles/second or 0.000593 percent.

The speed of light based on Timaeus is 186,171 miles/second.

c. Symmetrical Measures in the Solar System

There are some other measures using the international mile and the measure of the minute in seconds that have a striking symmetry and shake the foundations of the belief that they could result from mere coincidence. All three are multiples of the number of seconds in a day, half a day, and a fourth of a day.

- 86,400 seconds (1,440 minutes · 60 seconds) in a day
- 43,200 seconds in half a day
- 21,600 seconds in a quarter of a day

Again, using these numbers as root numbers—864, 432, and 216 respectively—these numbers correspond to several noteworthy linear measures in the solar system.

- 864,000 (compare w. diameter of the Sun in miles: 864,377)[10]
- 4,320 (compare w. diameter of Earth's core in miles: 4,325)[11]
- 2,160 (compare w. diameter of Earth's Moon in miles: 2,159.365)[12]

Humankind played no part in arranging these measures. If man knew the measures of time in the distant past, it wasn't until fairly recently that he had the technical wherewithal to measure these linear measures much less symmetrically coordinate them with the measures of time.

In summary, the numbers obtained from Timaeus's triangles directly and by derivation form the basis for establishing the dimensions of Earth and for all Earth's associated measures of time and distance. They also form the basis for those measures of the universe as well as Timaeus claimed.

---

[10] Ibid

[11] Wikipedia, "Structure of the Earth" https://en.wikipedia.org/wiki/Structure_of_Earth accessed November 11, 2021. Cited value derives from the table of values.

[12] Wikipedia, "List of Solar System objects by size," https://en.wikipedia.org/wiki/List_of_Solar_System_objects_by_size accessed November 11, 2021

CHAPTER 2

The Nature and Shape of the World

Timaeus is clear on the nature and shape of the world (universe) as is evident from his words on the subject. The creator fashioned the world, which he made into a globe or sphere, perfectly smooth and with every point on its surface equidistant from the center.

Now the creation took up the whole of each of the four elements; for the Creator compounded the world out of all the fire and all the water and all the air and all the earth, leaving no part of any of them nor any power of them outside. His intention was, in the first place, that the animal should be as far as possible a perfect whole and of perfect parts: [33] secondly, that it should be one, leaving no remnants out of which another such world might be created: and also that it should be free from old age and unaffected by disease. Considering that if heat and cold and other powerful forces which unite bodies surround and attack them from without when they are unprepared, they decompose them, and by bringing diseases and old age upon them, make them waste away—for this cause and on these grounds he made the world one whole, having every part entire, and being therefore perfect and not liable to old age and disease. And he gave to the world the figure which was suitable and also natural. Now to the animal which was to comprehend all animals, that figure was suitable which comprehends within itself all other figures. Wherefore he made the world in the form of a globe, round as from a lathe, having its extremes in every direction equidistant from the centre, the most perfect and the most like itself of all figures; for he considered that the like is infinitely fairer than the unlike. This he finished off, making the surface smooth all around for many reasons; in the first place, because the living being had no need of eyes when there was nothing remaining outside him to be seen; nor of ears when there was nothing to be heard; and there was no surrounding atmosphere to be breathed; nor would there have been any use of organs by the help of which he might receive his food or get rid of what he had already digested, since there was nothing which went from him or came into him: for there was nothing beside him. Of design he was created thus, his own waste providing his own food, and all that he did or suffered taking place in and by himself. For the Creator conceived that a being which was self-sufficient would be far more excellent than one which lacked anything; and, as he had no need to take anything or defend himself against any one, the Creator did not think it necessary to bestow upon him hands: nor had he any need of feet, [34] nor of the whole apparatus of walking; *but the movement suited to his spherical form was assigned to him, being of all the seven that which is most appropriate to mind and intelligence; and he was made to move in the same manner and on the same spot, within his own limits revolving in a circle. All the other six motions were taken away from him, and he was made not to partake of their deviations.* And as this circular movement required no feet, the universe was created without legs and without feet. (emphasis added)

Such was the whole plan of the eternal God about the god that was to be, to whom for this reason he gave a body, smooth and even, having a surface in every direction equidistant from the centre, a body entire and perfect, and formed out of perfect bodies. And in the centre he put the soul, which he diffused throughout the body, making it also to be the exterior environment of it; and he made the universe a circle moving in a circle, one and solitary, yet by reason of its excellence able to converse with itself, and needing no other friendship or acquaintance. Having these purposes in view he created the world a blessed god.

The movement of the globe of the world is interesting. From the emphasis in the foregoing passage, it is readily apparent that there are seven possible motions that could have been endowed on the creature. Six of them are the classic motions about the three axes (x, y, and z) of the Cartesian coordinate system. There is linear movement along each of the three axes and an angular or rotational movement around each of the three for a total of six. None of these six motions was given the creature; rather, he was assigned only the seventh, an orbital movement around a center. At the center of his creation, God placed the soul of the world, which was diffused throughout the globe to its limits and provided its exterior as well. And finally, "he made the universe a circle moving in a circle." This circle within a circle is the motion of the as-yet undifferentiated and incomplete solar system orbiting around a center against a backdrop of the stars of the upper heavens or the globe of the upper heavens. A perfect circle in a circle.

CHAPTER 3

Number—The Essence of Creation

This chapter is based on the most difficult of all passages in Timaeus. It is rendered especially difficult because of the numbers described and discussed in some detail. Simply reading this passage and discerning its meaning is quite difficult if not impossible without considerable reflection on and analysis of Timaeus's intent and meaning.

Timaeus's narrative here seems obtuse and unnecessarily difficult to follow. Was this purposeful, or was he struggling for words to describe the table? In my opinion, he doesn't seem to struggle, and his words flow easily, so his description had to have been intentional. And continuing in this vein, was he trying to be cryptic, and if so, toward what end? If his intent was to be cryptic, he would not be the first author to employ such a device to protect his intellectual work and to force others to struggle to discern his meaning. This is precisely the challenge intended for the uninitiated and students for whom understanding his words would be possible only if they studied and learned the necessary background material much as I did—a very time-consuming venture. However, finding the key and unlocking the puzzle if you will opens an immense trove of information, and having studied and learned the background material, I was better able to use Timaeus's words to understand other passages of his text.

a. Essence and Number

Timaeus's narrative is readily understood once you realize that he is describing a table, a form of the Cartesian coordinate system that incorporates a geometric progression that begins with 2 and 3 and continues with 2 and 3 as the intervals. It is a table in which many of the solar system's most important measures involving time and distance are present.

The numbers generated from this combination of 2 and 3 and from their intervals are not simply an exercise in mathematics; rather, the numbers, since they arise from the elements of creation, specifically define the measures of time and distance in the universe—a proposition the validity of which will become evident as this theme is developed.

Timaeus refers to numbers and measures as essence and describes it as an essential component of creation, one drawn from a combination of the other two components, soul and matter, with matter being composed of earth, wind, water, and fire. The soul is indivisible and unchangeable while matter is divisible. From soul (also called the "same") and matter (also called the "other"), the creator fashioned essence. Soul, matter, and essence were then combined by the creator, and from this combination, the creator delineated number and measure, which are specific components of creation. There is nothing arbitrary or happenstance in any of this; it is all by specific design.

Here then are Timaeus's words.

> Such was the whole plan of the eternal God about the god that was to be, to whom for this reason he gave a body, smooth and even, having a surface in every direction equidistant from the centre, a body entire and perfect, and formed out of perfect bodies. And in the centre he put the soul, which he diffused throughout the body, making it also to be the exterior environment of it; and he made the universe a circle moving in a circle, one and solitary, yet by reason of its excellence able to converse with itself, and needing no other friendship or acquaintance. Having these purposes in view he created the world a blessed god.

> Now God did not make the soul after the body, although we are speaking of them in this order; for having brought them together he would never have allowed that the elder should be ruled by the younger; but this is a random manner of speaking which we have, because somehow we ourselves too are very much under the dominion of chance. Whereas he made the soul in origin and excellence prior to and older than the body, to be the ruler and mistress, of whom the body was to be the subject. And he made her out of the following elements and on this wise: [35] Out of the indivisible and unchangeable, and also out of that which is divisible and has to do with material bodies, he compounded a third and intermediate kind of essence, partaking of the nature of the same and of the other, and this compound he placed accordingly in a mean between the indivisible, and the divisible and material. He took the three elements of the same, the other, and the essence, and mingled them into one form, compressing by force the reluctant and unsociable nature of the other into the same. When he had mingled them with the essence and out of three made one, he again divided this whole into as many portions as was fitting, each portion being a compound of the same, the other, and the essence. And he proceeded to divide after this manner:—First of all, he took away one part of the whole [1], and then he separated a second part which was double the first [2], and then he

took away a third part which was half as much again as the second and three times as much as the first [3], and then he took a fourth part which was twice as much as the second [4], and a fifth part which was three times the third [9], and a sixth part which was eight times the first [8], and a seventh part which was twenty-seven times the first [27]. After this he filled up the double intervals [i.e. between 1, 2, 4, 8] and [36] the triple [i.e. between 1, 3, 9, 27] cutting off yet other portions from the mixture and placing them in the intervals, so that in each interval there were two kinds of means, the one exceeding and exceeded by equal parts of its extremes [as for example 1, 4/3, 2, in which the mean 4/3 is one-third of 1 more than 1, and one-third of 2 less than 2], the other being that kind of mean which exceeds and is exceeded by an equal number. Where there were intervals of 3/2 and of 4/3 and of 9/8, made by the connecting terms in the former intervals, he filled up all the intervals of 4/3 with the interval of 9/8, leaving a fraction over; and the interval which this fraction expressed was in the ratio of 256 to 243. And thus the whole mixture out of which he cut these portions was all exhausted by him.

b. The Table and Its Numbers

The table thus constructed from Timaeus's words is as follows.

X 2↓ X 3 →

1	3	9	27	81	243	729	2,187	6,561
2	6	18	54	162	486	1,458	4,374	13,122
4	12	36	108	324	972	2,916	8,748	26,244
8	24	72	216	648	1,944	5,832	17,496	52,488
16	48	144	432	1,296	3,888	11,664	34,992	104,976
32	96	288	864	2,592	7,776	23,328	69,984	209,952
64	192	576	1,728	5,184	15,552	46,656	139,968	419,904
128	384	1,152	3,456	10,368	31,104	93,312	279,936	839,808
256	768	2,304	6,912	20,736	62,208	186,624	559,872	1,679,616
512	1,536	4,608	13,824	41,472	124,416	373,248	1,119,744	3,359,232

Figure 4

Timaeus's progression

The "double intervals" are those generated by multiplying each number starting with 2 by 2 (Timaeus's "mean"), which produces the progression seen in the table's vertical column. The "triple intervals" are those generated by multiplying each number starting with 3 by 3 (Timaeus's "mean"), which produces the progression seen in the table's horizontal row. An interval of 6 is also present though it is not mentioned by Timaeus. This interval, which begins with the number 6, continues diagonally with each number being the product of its predecessor multiplied by 6 ("mean"), ex., 6, 36, 216, 1,296, etc. Collectively, these means with their "equal numbers" are the second category of means that Timaeus describes.

The first mean described by Timaeus is "the one exceeding and exceeded by equal parts of its extremes." (I have intentionally left off the annotation that appears in the text in brackets. I don't know by whom or when it was added, but it is erroneous.) This statement by Timaeus is another of his cryptic statements that can be readily understood when the key is provided. In this case, Timaeus is describing the process for determining the relationship of a specific number in the table to the vertical and horizontal progressions of 2 and 3 respectively. In this, he anticipates Renè Descartes and his eponymous Cartesian coordinate system by many centuries.

For example, the number 2,592 is a product of 81 (from the row of 3) and 32 (from the column of 2. The numbers 81 and 32 are the extremes, and the means are either 32 for the extreme of 81 or 81 for the extreme of 32. In other words, if the extreme is 32, the mean is 81, and if the extreme is 81, the mean is 32. Both are equal—one and the same. The term *means* is spoken to in an earlier passage from Timaeus.

> And the fairest bond is that which makes the most complete fusion of itself and the things which it combines; and proportion is best adapted to effect such a union. For whenever in any three numbers, whether cube or square, there is a mean, which is to the last term what the first term is to it; [32] and again, when the mean is to the first term as the last term is to the mean—then the mean becoming first and last, and the first and last both becoming means, they will all of them of necessity come to be the same, and having become the same with one another will be all one.

While it provides additional description of means, this passage is just as cryptic as the earlier one cited though it is saying the same thing. However, Timaeus's use of the terms *extremes* and *means* is simply a technique he employs for determining the exact location of each number in the table that is formed by the combined geometric progressions of 2 and 3 by specifying its extremes. Whether we locate 2,592 by specifying its extremes in the table as 81 · 32 or 32 · 81 is immaterial; both are the same, and both equal 2,592.

c. Fractions and Ratios

Recognizing the risk of further confusing this whole matter, at this point, we must discuss the several intervals as well as the associated terms *fraction* and *ratio* that Timaeus introduces at

[36], which immediately follow his discussion of the intervals of 2 and 3. These intervals all have the appearance of fractions including the fraction or ratio he cites; they are 3/2, 4/3, 9/8 and 256/243. The key to his meaning here can be found in his own words.

> Where there were intervals of 3/2 and of 4/3 and of 9/8, *made by connecting the terms in the former intervals, he filled up* all the intervals of 4/3 with the interval 9/8, leaving a fraction over; and the interval which this fraction expressed was in the ratio of 256 to 243. (emphasis added)

These fractions are nothing more than coordinates that described successively expanding rectangular areas of the table shown at figure 4 beginning at the upper left-hand corner. The "former intervals" referred to in the above quoted passage refers to the first mean. The coordinates 3/2 incorporate numbers 1, 2, 3, and 6. The coordinates 4/3 incorporate the numbers incorporated by 3/2 as well as the numbers 4 and 12. The coordinates 9/8 incorporate those numbers incorporated by 3/2 and 4/3 as well as the numbers 18, 24, 36, and 72. (See figure 5 following. Note that the connecting terms 3/2 and 4/3 are included in the unshaded areas.) Then if one refers to the table, the coordinates 256/243 incorporate those same numbers incorporated by 3/2 and 4/3 and 9/8 respectively but also many more. All that these coordinates do then is further flesh out or fill up the table; they serve no other purpose.

1	3	9
2	6	18
4	12	36
8	24	72

Figure 5

Filling up the intervals by connecting the terms 9/8

All of this is very complicated, but what must be recognized is that Timaeus is describing the table at figure 4—nothing more, nothing less. This table creates a harmonious pattern from which God delineated the universe and gave it number and measure. It is as Timaeus stated one of the three fundamental parts that God used to make the universe. Between [26] and [27], he states,

> And for these reasons, and out of such elements which are in number four [earth, wind, fire, and water], the body of the world was created, and it was harmonized by proportion and therefore has the spirit of friendship; and having been reconciled to itself, it was indissoluble by the hand of any other than the framer.

We are near the beginning of creation here but not quite there. Earlier in his narrative, Timaeus states,

> Let me tell you then why the creator made this world of generation. He was good, and the good can never have any jealousy of anything. And being free from jealousy, he desired that all things should be as like himself as they could be. This is in the truest sense the origin of creation and of the world, [30] as we shall do well in believing on the testimony of wise men: God desired that all things should be good and nothing bad, so far as this was attainable.

d. The Pattern and Its Ramifications in Measure

Having discussed at length in this chapter the origins and nature of the table created by Timaeus's geometric progressions of 2 and 3 and having found it a harmonious whole, let us now examine its particulars for their relevance to the actual measures of time and distance.

The table earlier depicted as figure 4 is reproduced below for ease of reference. From this point on, we will refer to the table as the pattern, a name that Timaeus uses in [28], [37], and [38]. However, before we proceed with a more in-depth discussion of the pattern, it is important that we digress for a moment to clarify the nature of the pattern and its relationship to the visible universe. I am jumping ahead of the tale by raising the issue of time here instead of waiting to raise it at its logical point in the narrative, but it is important that I do so. Timaeus at [28].

> The work of the creator, whenever he looks to the unchangeable and fashions the form and nature of his work after an unchangeable pattern, must necessarily be made fair and perfect, but when he looks to the created only, and uses a created pattern, it is not fair or perfect.

The pattern that Timaeus lays out in this table is perfect since it exists in eternity. Timaeus states at [38],

> Time, then, and the heaven came into being at the same instant in order that, having been created together, if ever there was to be a dissolution of them, they might be dissolved together. *It was framed after the pattern of the eternal nature, that it might resemble this as far as was possible; for the pattern exists from eternity,* and the created heaven has been, and is, and will be, in all time. (emphasis added)

The pattern is perfect, but what of the created universe? As Timaeus notes at [37], it is not though it has the appearance of being so. If it were perfect, the world would also be perfect, and it is not. Timaeus wrote,

When the father creator saw the creature which he had made moving and living, the created image of the eternal gods, he rejoiced, and in his joy determined to make the copy still more like the original; and as this was eternal, he sought to make the universe eternal, so far as might be. *Now the nature of the ideal being was everlasting, but to bestow this attribute in its fulness upon a creature was impossible. Wherefore he resolved to have a moving image of eternity, and when he set in order the heaven, he made this image eternal but moving according to number, while eternity itself rests in unity; and this image we call time.* For there were no days and nights and months and years before the heaven was created, but when he constructed the heaven he created them also. They are all parts of time, and the past and future are created species of time, which we unconsciously but wrongly transfer to the eternal essence. (emphasis added)

Further discussion and analysis of the pattern.

1	3	9	27	81	243	729	2,187	6,561
2	6	18	54	162	486	1,458	4,374	13,122
4	12	36	108	324	972	2,916	8,748	26,244
8	24	72	216	648	1,944	5,832	17,496	52,488
16	48	144	432	1,296	3,888	11,664	34,992	104,976
32	96	288	864	2,592	7,776	23,328	69,984	209,952
64	192	576	1,728	5,184	15,552	46,656	139,968	419,904
128	384	1,152	3,456	10,368	31,104	93,312	279,936	839,808
256	768	2,304	6,912	20,736	62,208	186,624	559,872	1,679,616
512	1,536	4,608	13,824	41,472	124,416	373,248	1,119,744	3,359,232

Each number I cite from this table is located by a set of coordinates, which I call a pattern pair. (I would use Timaeus's terms of means, extremes, and intervals as defined earlier, but they are too cumbersome and potentially confusing). For example, 864 is located by the pattern pair (27/32). After each such citation, I will describe its significance to a specific measure of time and distance and then cite its actual measure. These numbers are presented as significant measures from the pattern; there are many others that could be cited too.

e. Pattern Numbers and Measures in the Created Universe

The pattern has number, but something critical is missing: the terms of the measures that derive from number—minute, mile, degree of arc, orbital revolutions, years, etc. Where are these in the text? Timaeus does not specify them except for day/night, month, and year. However, the terms of measure too must be a part of creation; otherwise, number is rendered largely meaningless. The terms of measure must have been provided for at the creation, but how I cannot say, and Timaeus is largely silent on this most important point. There is another possibility: only some of the terms were made available at the creation; the rest were learned over the many eons of time since creation. However, all are derived from the pattern.

Below is a small sample of the measures that can be found in the pattern.

6 (3/2) Significance: 60 is the number of minutes/hour, and the number of seconds/minute. Actual measurement: 60.

18 (9/2) Significance: 18 years is the number of tropical years in saros eclipse cycle. Actual measure: 18.03 years.[13]

24 (3/8) Significance: 24 hours is the number of hours in a day. Actual measure: 24 hours.

36 (9/4) Significance: 360 is the number of degrees in a circle. Actual measure: 360 degrees.

54 (27/2) Significance: 54 is the number of tropical years in exeligmos eclipse cycle. Actual measure: 54.1 years.[14]

72 (9/8) Significance: 72 is the average number of saros series members in the average series. Actual number: 71–73.[15]

144 (9/16) Significance: 1,440 is the number of minutes in a day. Actual number: 1,440 minutes.

216 (27/8) Significance: 2,160 miles is the diameter of the Moon. Actual measure: 2,159 miles.[16]

243 (243/) Significance: 243 is the number of years in a Venus transit cycle. Actual measure: 243 years.[17]

432 (27/16) Significance: 4,320 miles in the diameter of Earth's electromagnetic core. Actual figure: 4,325 miles.

5832 (729/8) Significance: 583.2 days in octaeteris cycle; also, the Venus inferior conjunction cycle in days. Actual measure: 584 days.[18]

---

[13] Wikipedia, "Saros (Astronomy)," https://en.wikipedia.org/wiki/Saros_(astronomy) accessed Feb. 27, 2021.

[14] Wikipedia, "Exeligmos." https://en.wikipedia.org/wiki/Exeligmos accessed November 11, 2021

[15] Fred Espenak and Jean Meus, *Five Millennium Canon of Lunar Eclipses—1,999 to +3,000 (2,000 BCE to 3,000 CE)*, National Aeronautics and Space Administration pub. NASA/TP-209-214172, January 2009, 59. Can be viewed online at NASA's Eclipse Web Site Five Millennium Canon of Lunar Eclipses: -1999 to +3000 (nasa.gov). accessed November 11, 2021. See link to canon under supplementary data. Reference text pp 60-61

[16] Wikipedia, "Moon," https://en.wikipedia.org/wiki/Moon accessed February 27, 2021. See "Physical Characteristics" in column to the right.

[17] NASA Eclipse Web Site, "Six millennium catalogue of Venus Transits: 2,000 BCE to 4,000 CE," NASA - Catalog of Transits of Venus accessed November 11, 2021

[18] Wikipedia, "Octaeteris," https://en.wikipedia.org/wiki/Octaeteris accessed February 27, 2021.

864 (27/32) Significance: 864,000 miles in the diameter of the Sun and the number of seconds in a day. Actual diameter of Sun: 864,377 miles.

1,296 (81/16) Significance: 1,296 years in the average life of a saros eclipse series. Actual measure: 1,298 years based on an average of 72 eclipses/series with 18.03 years between eclipses in the series.[19]

25,920 (81/32) Significance: time in years that it takes for Earth's axis to precess 360 degrees. Actual figure is estimated to be approximately 26,000 years.[20]

93,312 (729/128) Significance: 93,312,000 is the number of miles in the astronomical unit. Actual measure: 92,956,000 miles.[21] This is approximately the semi-minor axis measure of Earth's distance to the Sun.

186,624 (729/256) Significance: 186,624 miles/second is the speed of light. Actual measure is 186,235 miles/second.[22]

While it may seem that the numbers in this table with their close relationship to actual measures are there simply by coincidence, this is not the case; these numbers were used in the creation of the universe as Timaeus states. As the essence of creation, they were incorporated into the original design of the universe.

A final question: Who designed and compiled this table from which these numbers, which pervade all creation, were taken? It can be no other than God, who designed the table, a perfect pattern that rests in eternity just as Timaeus states.

Now that there is soul, matter, and essence—the three elements of creation—the architect of all will create the universe, and we will bear witness to this as Timaeus proceeds with the telling.

---

[19] Espenak and Meus, <u>Five Millennium Canon of Lunar Eclipses: -1999 to +3000 (nasa.gov)</u> pp 60-61.

[20] Wikipedia, "Axial Precession," https://en.wikipedia.org/wiki/Axial_precession accessed February 22, 2021.

[21] Wikipedia, "Astronomical Unit," https://en.wikipedia.org/wiki/Astronomical_unit accessed Feb. 27, 2021.

[22] Wikipedia "Speed of light," https://en.wikipedia.org/wiki/Speed_of_light accessed February 27, 2021.

CHAPTER 4

Geometry and Creation

The universe began with the three elements of creation that were combined and thoroughly mixed, and this mixture was then arranged by geometry. Thus begins the visible universe that can be reflected upon and comprehended with reason.

And thus, the whole mixture out of which he cut these portions was all exhausted by him. This entire compound he divided lengthways into two parts, which he joined to one another at the centre like the letter X, and bent them into a circular form, connecting them with themselves and each other at the point opposite to their original meeting-point; and, comprehending them in a uniform revolution upon the same axis, he made the one the outer and the other the inner circle. Now the motion of the outer circle he called the motion of the same, and the motion of the inner circle the motion of the other or diverse. The motion of the same he carried round by the side to the right, and the motion of the diverse diagonally to the left. And he gave dominion to the motion of the same and like, for that he left single and undivided; but the inner motion he divided in six places and made seven unequal circles having their intervals in ratios of two-and three, three of each, and bade the orbits proceed in a direction opposite to one another; and three [Sun, Mercury, Venus] he made to move with equal swiftness, and the remaining four [Moon, Saturn, Mars, Jupiter] to move with unequal swiftness to the three and to one another, but in due proportion.

Now when the Creator had framed the soul according to his will, he formed within her the corporeal universe, and brought the two together, and united them centre to centre. The soul interfused everywhere from the centre to the circumference of heaven, of which also she is the external envelopment, herself turning in herself, began a divine beginning of never ceasing and rational life enduring throughout all time. [37] The body of heaven is visible, but the soul is invisible, and partakes of reason and harmony, and being made by the best of intellectual and everlasting natures, is the best of things created. And because she is composed of the same and of the other and of the essence, these three, and is divided and united in due proportion, and in her revolutions returns upon herself, the soul, when touching anything which has essence, whether dispersed in parts or undivided, is stirred through all her powers, to declare the sameness or difference of that thing and some other; and to what individuals are related, and by what affected, and in what way and how and when, both in the world of generation and in the world of immutable being. And when reason, which works with equal truth, whether she be in the circle of the diverse or of the same—in voiceless silence holding her onward course in the sphere of the self-moved—when reason, I say, is hovering around the sensible world and when the circle of the diverse also moving truly imparts the intimations of sense to the whole soul, then arise opinions and beliefs sure and certain. But when reason is concerned with the rational, and the circle of the same moving smoothly declares it, then intelligence and knowledge are necessarily perfected. And if anyone affirms that in which these two are found to be other than the soul, he will say the very opposite of the truth.

a. Vesica Pisces—The Crucible of Creation

It is not known by whom or when the several annotations that appear in brackets in the text were made, but they are erroneous and should be ignored. The text that appears at the beginning of the above quote describes a well-known geometric figure named the Vesica Pisces, Latin for "fish bladder." This is an unfortunate name as the figure is of profound significance to creation. With a close rereading of the cited text and by following its words exactly, the image of the Vesica Pisces is created. (See figure 6 below.)

And thus, the whole mixture out of which he cut these portions was all exhausted by him. This entire compound he divided lengthways into two parts, which he joined to one another at the centre like the letter X, and bent them into a circular form, connecting them with themselves and each other at the point opposite to their original meeting-point.

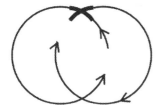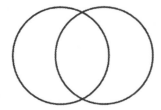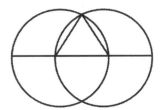

Figure 6

The Origin of the Vesica Pisces

Note from the first drawing how the two lines are overlapped to create an X as the text states and how the lines are then bent around to their opposite intersection at a similar X. The middle drawing depicts the completed Vesica Pisces while the last shows the image of the equilateral triangle that can readily be drawn at the almond shape (in Italian, "mandorla") center of the Vesica Pisces, where the two circles overlap one another. This third drawing was Euclid's First Proposition demonstrating that the triangle formed at this union of the two circles is equilateral. Note further that the figure of the Vesica Pisces embodies the same 3-2 numbers of the pattern in its broad dimensions, which are breadth, 3 half-circles, and height, 2 half-circles.

The Vesica Pisces is the beginning of the visible universe, the crucible in which God gave the universe form and dimension. The image of the Vesica Pisces is immediately evocative of a human, female vagina at the moment of birth. This is not a coincidence, and we are privileged to view the geometric image of the chamber of creation in which God has given females the privilege to share in his power of creation. There is no more sacred image than this; it is the holy of holies.

b. Creation of the Four Platonic Solids

The equilateral triangle that arises from the Vesica Pisces is the first created image. While it is only two dimensional, the next statement in the text following the description of the Vesica Pisces states, "and, comprehending them in a uniform revolution upon the same axis, he made the one the outer and the other the inner circle."

The axis is not defined, but it seems reasonable to assume that all three axes are implied, i.e., x, y, and z axes in a three-dimensional Cartesian coordinate system. If this is the case, then "a uniform revolution upon the same axis" implies that a sphere is generated from this motion. In other words, by rotating the entire image, a sphere within a sphere is created with the outermost edge of each circle defining an outer sphere and the center overlapping almond shape defining an inner sphere. However, if only one axis is used, for example the vertical or y axis, the outer edges of the image define an outer circle while the almond shape defines an inner circle.

Considering the equilateral triangle that is formed in the almond shape if this image is rotated through 360 degrees of the inner circle with its progress marked in 120-degree increments; then, the image that is defined is the first Platonic solid, the tetrahedron. If its progress is marked in 90-degree increments and its mirror image is inscribed in the lower half of the almond shape, producing a diamond shape, the second Platonic solid, the octahedron, is defined. And if the diamond shape from the octahedron is rotated and its progress is marked in 72-degree increments, instead, and this entire image is copied then inserted into its interstices, a net of twenty equilateral triangles is formed[23] (see figure 7 below), which produces the icosahedron, the third Platonic solid. (The net image is a convenient way of showing the relationship between the equilateral triangle and the icosahedron and does not suggest that the net was an intermediate step in creating the icosahedron though it could have been.)

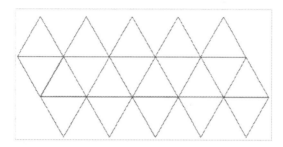

Figure 7

Icosahedron net

The significance of almond shape then is that it can produce the first three of the Platonic solids mentioned by Timaeus as detailed in chapter 1, but its internal structures also include the golden rectangle, which arises from a square that can readily be projected into a cube, the fourth of the Platonic solids in Timaeus. The significance of the icosahedron has already been discussed in chapter 1.

Another part of this text remains to be discussed, but its subject matter is such that it would best to cover it in its own chapter, which immediately follows.

---

[23] Wikipedia, "Regular Icosahedron," <u>Regular icosahedron - Wikipedia</u>. See the image of the net in the right column; accessed March 4, 2021.

CHAPTER 5

The Solar System Is Laid Out

This chapter arises from a portion of Timaeus's text that was quoted at the beginning of the previous chapter. This text was not analyzed or discussed in the previous chapter because it is quite involved and it covers a subject matter that mandates it be accorded its own chapter to treat it properly.

> Now the motion of the outer circle he called the motion of the same, and the motion of the inner circle the motion of the other or diverse. The motion of the same he carried round by the side to the right, and the motion of the diverse diagonally to the left. And he gave dominion to the motion of the same and like, for that he left single and undivided; but the inner motion he divided in six places and made seven unequal circles having their intervals in ratios of two-and three, three of each, and bade the orbits proceed in a direction opposite to one another; and three [Sun, Mercury, Venus] he made to move with equal swiftness, and the remaining four [Moon, Saturn, Mars, Jupiter] to move with unequal swiftness to the three and to one another, but in due proportion.

As noted in the previous chapter, it is not known by whom or when the annotations in the text that appear in brackets were made, but they are erroneous and should be ignored.

The equilateral triangle formed from the almond shape created by the overlapping of the two circles of the Vesica Pisces is the beginning of this discussion. The equilateral triangle is a part of the inner circle, which as described in the previous chapter was formed from the rotation of the almond shape. This "inner [motion] he divided in six places and makes seven unequal circles having their intervals in ratios of two and three, three of each," but how are these intervals defined, and what are the factors 2 and 3 predicated on—2 times what, and 3 times what? The equilateral triangle provides the answers to both questions. The center point of the equilateral triangle is marked by the intersection of six lines as shown in figure 8 following.

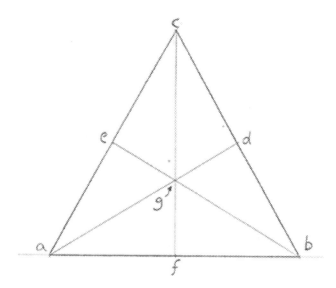

Figure 8

The equilateral triangle of the Vesica Pisces and Timaeus's six divisions

The six divisions are created by the following line segments: ac, cb, ba, cf, da, and eb. These six divisions create a number of right triangles each of which is a 30°–60°–90° triangle. The hypotenuse of each such triangle is equal to twice its lesser side, and the greater side is √3 times the lesser side. This relationship is the same no matter the scale of the triangle. For example, line segments cf and af, fb, ae, bd, cd, and ec are all √3 even though the scale of cf is three times the others, which are all equal.

If line segment af is equal to √3, line segment cf is equal to (√3)² or 3. Then line segment cg is twice the length of line segment gf; and point g is 1/3 of the height line segment cf, or 1 of 3. This is a critical relationship as it determines one of the basic measures of the solar system, the astronomical unit, the mean distance of Earth to the Sun, approximately 93 million miles.

Accordingly, point f depicts the relative location of the Sun, point g depicts the relative position of Earth—thus, defining the AU measure as one—and point c depicts the relative position of the dwarf planet Ceres (the largest object in the asteroid belt) or approximately 3 AU.

If Ceres is at 3 AU, or properly speaking (√3 · √3) AU, half of that distance locates Mars at 1.5 AU, and half of that distance locates Venus at .75 AU, and half of that distance locates Mercury at .375 AU. (The interval ½ is a species of the number of 2.). These three planets make up those three circles with an interval of ½.

Again, with Ceres at (√3 · √3), then √3 times that distance locates Jupiter at 5.2 AU and √3 times that distance locates Saturn at 9 AU. (The interval √3 is a species of the number 3.) These three planets make up those circles with an interval of √3 . (NOTE: Ceres is <u>not</u> counted twice. Although Ceres is at (√3 · √3) or 3 AU, the number 3 is a determining factor for the three inner planets (Mars, Venus, and Mercury), which are at the ½ interval. Ceres, with an interval of ($\sqrt{3}$ · $\sqrt{3}$) is a member of the three outer planets (Ceres, Jupiter, and Saturn), which are at the $\sqrt{3}$ interval.)

However, if Jupiter and Saturn are to be included in the equilateral triangle shown at figure 8, the scale must be changed by a factor of three. In this case, point g would be the position occupied by Ceres (3 AU), and point c would be the position occupied by Saturn (9 AU) with Jupiter at an intermediate position defined as $\sqrt{3}$ · 3, or 5.2 AU.

This entire plot is heliocentric. It does not provide for Earth's Moon or any other planetary moons in the solar system, which cannot be assigned a meaningful AU value. The other planets, Uranus and Neptune, are not provided for since Timaeus mentions only seven circles and these two planets would make a total of nine. Were Uranus and Neptune intentionally excluded from this plot because their respective AU values do not fit either of Timaeus's two interval factors, ½ or $\sqrt{3}$—which they do not by wide margins? Alternatively, were they not provided for because their existence was not known at the time—a technological limitation? I cannot offer a definitive answer, but I suspect that because they do not fit the pattern, they were not included, but their not fitting the pattern raises several questions. How far or how widely does the pattern extend in the wider cosmos? Similarly, did the creator intend only for it to define the design of Earth and those objects in its vicinity in the solar system? Does the pattern attenuate with distance from Earth or from our ability to reason? Profound questions. Perhaps the answer can be found at Timaeus [31].

> This being supposed, let us proceed to the next stage: In the likeness of what animal did the Creator make the world? It would be an unworthy thing to liken it to any nature which exists as a part only; for nothing can be beautiful which is like any imperfect thing; but let us suppose the world to be the very image of that whole of which all other animals both individually and in their tribes are portions. For the original of the universe contains in itself all intelligible beings, just as this world comprehends us and all other visible creatures. For the Deity, intending to make this world like the fairest and most perfect of intelligible beings, framed one visible animal comprehending within itself all other animals of a kindred nature. [31]. Are we right in saying that there is one world, or that they are many and infinite? There must be one only, if the created copy is to accord with the original. For that which includes all other intelligible creatures cannot have a second or companion; in that case there would be need of another living being which would include both, and of which they would be parts, and the likeness would be more truly said to resemble not them, but that other which included them. In order then that the world might be solitary, like the perfect animal, the creator made

not two worlds or an infinite number of them; but there is and ever will be one only-begotten and created heaven.

Had this passage ended with the word *world* instead of *heaven*, we might have satisfactory answers to our questions or at least a hint of where to proceed with them, but at best, this passage is ambiguous. Regretfully, we must leave this issue for now as it cannot be easily resolved and to pursue it any further would be a distraction.

There is an important matter still outstanding for us to address—How closely do the Timaeus values for planetary AU distances accord with current values of planetary AU distances? Consider the following table (All values are from NASA's Planetary Fact Sheet[24] except for those of Ceres.[25])

	Mercury	Venus	Earth	Mars	Ceres	Jupiter	Saturn
AU distance (Timaeus)	.375	.75	1	1.5	3	5.2	9
AU distance, mean	.387	.723	1	1.52	2.77	5.2	9.58
AU at perihelion*	.313	.731	1	1.41	2.6	5.03	9.2
AU at aphelion**	.459	.716	1	1.64	3	5.37	9.96

NOTES: *Perihelion is the planet's closest orbital distance to the Sun. **Aphelion is the planet's furthest orbital distance from the Sun.

Figure 9

Astronomical unit (AU) distances compared

Timaeus's values when compared to the current AU mean values are fairly close for Mercury, Venus, Mars, and Jupiter but less so for Ceres and Saturn. Timaeus's value for Ceres's distance falls within Ceres's orbital range and matches its aphelion distance. Timaeus's value for Saturn's distance is fairly close to Saturn's distance at perihelion but otherwise is a poor match. All in all though, Timaeus's AU values are closer to the real values than not. However, it must be remembered that Timaeus's values are design values and may or may not accord very well with current actual values. The design values are of course the creator's, and they are as nearly perfect as a copy of the original can be while the created values are not perfect. In any case, the modern values of planetary distances as created are presumed to be as accurate as modern science can make them and are accepted as such without hesitation or reservation.

Kepler's Third Law, worked out over years of careful observation and many long hours of

---

[24] National Aeronautics and Space Administration (NASA) Web Site, "Planetary Fact Sheet, Ratio to Earth Values (U.S. Units)" Planetary Fact Sheet - Ratio to Earth (nasa.gov). accessed November 11, 2021

[25] Wikipedia, "Ceres (dwarf planet)," Ceres (dwarf planet) - Wikipedia.; accessed March 4, 2021. See column on right "Orbital Characteristics"

contemplation and reflection and articulated in 1609 to 1619, also appears to be part of the creator's design using factors of 2 and 3. Kepler's Third Law states, "The square of a planet's orbital period is proportional to the cube of the length of the semi-major axis of its orbit."[26]

Using Jupiter as an example,

Jupiter's orbital period (T) is: 4,332 days/365.25 days = $(11.86)^2$ = 140.67.
Jupiter's AU (R) is 5.2 = $(5.2)^3$ = 140.608.
Jupiter's R/Jupiter's T = 140.67/140.6 = 1.

It is noteworthy that one value (T) is squared while the second is cubed, or two and three respectively. The fact that this law may be part of the creator's design does not diminish Kepler's great achievement in discovering this relationship, and he is appropriately celebrated for it.

Thus far, we have discussed those steps in creation that occurred before there was motion, before time began. Next, we will follow the creator as he initiates time.

---

[26] Wikipedia, "Kepler's laws of planetary motion," Kepler's laws of planetary motion - Wikipedia, accessed March 5, 2021.

CHAPTER 6

A Moving Image of Eternity—Time Begins

The circle was the original figure in creation, the first manifestation of soul and reason in the created universe. From this, we have seen how the creator combined soul and matter with essence to create dimension and number, and from this mixture, he created the inner circle—the solar system—of heaven, and the outer circle—the stars of the broader cosmos—of heaven.

In the previous chapter, Timaeus stated that the creator assigned to the outer circle the motion of the same (in present times called prograde or more commonly direct motion) and to the inner circle the motion of the other or diverse (in present times called retrograde motion). All the planets of the solar system and some planetary moons revolve in retrograde motion, but this is not their constant motion as they also move in the same motion for long periods of time. As viewed from Earth, all planets appear to move in retrograde motion at some point in their orbits, some more so than others.

In its proper sequence, this discussion should have occurred in the previous chapter wherein the creation and spacing of the planets was discussed. I purposefully skipped this aspect of Timaeus's narrative earlier because it clearly states that the creator had assigned the planets their motion when he created them, but in subsequent text as cited immediately following, Timaeus states,

> When the father creator saw the creature which he had made *moving and living,* he rejoiced, and in his joy ... resolved to have *a moving image of eternity,* and when he set in order the heaven, he made this image eternal but moving according to number while eternity itself rests in unity, and this image we call time. (emphasis added)

A textual contradiction: either God created motion and time when he created the solar system, or he paused to reflect on the created solar system and then decided to create motion and time. So which is it? Just as important, does it matter? Then again, perhaps neither question is appropriate, and we should merely observe that God does not exist in time—never has, never will—we do; therefore, creation was not a series of discrete, chronologically sequential acts measured in time. However, Timaeus, in the telling of his story, needs to relate it as discrete and chronologically sequential acts, and we, his audience, need this format as well to logically follow it. Regardless, Timaeus resolves the issue stating in text subsequent to that earlier quoted, "For there were no days and nights and months and years before the heaven was created, but when he constructed the heaven he created them also."

The quoted text that follows is likely the most insightful ever written on the nature of God and time. It is well worth careful reading and reflection.

> When the father creator saw the creature which he had made moving and living, the created image of the eternal gods, he rejoiced, and in his joy determined to make the copy still more like the original; and as this was eternal, he sought to make the universe eternal, so far as might be. Now the nature of the ideal being was everlasting, but to bestow this attribute in its fulness upon a creature was impossible. Wherefore he resolved to have a moving image of eternity, and when he set in order the heaven, he made this image eternal but moving according to number, while eternity itself rests in unity; and this image we call time. For there were no days and nights and months and years before the heaven was created, but when he constructed the heaven he created them also. They are all parts of time, and the past and future are created species of time, which we unconsciously but wrongly transfer to the eternal essence; for we say that he "was," he "is," he "will be," but the truth is that "is" alone is properly attributed to him, [38] and that "was" and "will be" only to be spoken of becoming in time, for they are motions, but that which is immovably the same cannot become older or younger by time, nor ever did or has become, or hereafter will be, older or younger, nor is subject at all to any of those states which affect moving and sensible things and of which generation is the cause. These are the forms of time, which imitates eternity and revolves according to a law of number. Moreover, when we say that what has become is become and what becomes is becoming, and that what will become is about to become and that the non-existent is non-existent—all these are inaccurate modes of expression. But perhaps this whole subject will be more suitably discussed on some other occasion.

In the following text, Timaeus describes the creation of movement and time and the measures of time. Here, we encounter a geocentric plot of the solar system, a Copernican no-no, but it is still the most useful and readily understandable way of discussing and measuring the various cycles of time.

Our perceptions of the Sun and Moon and planets orbiting Earth are very useful in this regard. Timaeus describes how the creator placed the seven stars in seven orbits, and while he names only the first four in the order Moon, Sun, Hermes (Mercury), and Lucifer (Venus), he declines naming the remaining three—likely Mars, Jupiter, and Saturn. But wait … Wasn't there another planet, Ceres, mentioned in the previous chapter? Yes there was, but Timaeus does not mention it here perhaps because it does not factor in any known time cycle. This is hardly a satisfactory answer, but I cannot provide another, and this is apparently Timaeus's as well as he states in the emphasized text following: *"Now, when all the stars which were necessary to the creation of time had attained a motion suitable to them—and had become living creatures having bodies fastened by vital chains …"*

Time, then, and the heaven came into being at the same instant in order that, having been created together, if ever there was to be a dissolution of them, they might be dissolved together. It was framed after the pattern of the eternal nature, that it might resemble this as far as was possible; for the pattern exists from eternity, and the created heaven has been, and is, and will be, in all time. Such was the mind and thought of God in the creation of time. The sun and moon and five other stars, which are called the planets, were created by him in order to distinguish and preserve the numbers of time; and when he had made—their several bodies, he placed them in the orbits in which the circle of the other was revolving—in seven orbits seven stars. First, there was the moon in the orbit nearest the earth, and next the sun, in the second orbit above the earth; then came the morning star and the star sacred to Hermes, moving in orbits which have an equal swiftness with the sun, but in an opposite direction; and this is the reason why the sun and Hermes and Lucifer overtake and are overtaken by each other. To enumerate the places which he assigned to the other stars, and to give all the reasons why he assigned them, although a secondary matter, would give more trouble than the primary. These things at some future time, when we are at leisure, may have the consideration which they deserve, but not at present.

Now, when all the stars which were necessary to the creation of time had attained a motion suitable to them,—and had become living creatures having bodies fastened by vital chains, and learnt their appointed task, [39] moving in the motion of the diverse, which is diagonal, and passes through and is governed by the motion of the same, they revolved, some in a larger and some in a lesser orbit—those which had the lesser orbit revolving faster, and those which had the larger more slowly. Now by reason of the motion of the same, those which revolved fastest appeared to be overtaken by those which moved slower although they really overtook them; for the motion of the same made them all turn in a spiral, and, because some went one way and some another, that which receded most slowly from the sphere of the same, which was the swiftest, appeared to follow it most nearly. That there might be some visible measure of their relative swiftness and slowness as they proceeded in their *eight courses*, God lighted a fire, which we now call the sun, in the second from the earth of these orbits, that it might give light to the whole of heaven, and that the animals, as many as nature intended, might participate in number, learning arithmetic from the revolution of the same and the like. Thus then, and for this reason the night and the day were created, being the period of the one most intelligent revolution. And the month is accomplished when the moon has completed her orbit and overtaken the sun, and the year when the sun has completed his own orbit. Mankind, with hardly an exception, have not remarked the periods of the other stars, and they have no name for them, and do not measure them against one another by the help of number, and hence they can scarcely be said to know that their wanderings, being infinite in number and admirable for their variety, make up time. And yet there is no difficulty in seeing that the perfect number of time fulfils the perfect year when all the *eight revolutions*, having their relative degrees of swiftness, are accomplished together and attain their completion at the same time, measured by the rotation of the same and equally moving. After this manner, and for these reasons, came into being such of the stars as in their heavenly progress received reversals of motion, to the end that the created heaven might imitate the eternal nature, and be as like as possible to the perfect and intelligible animal. (emphasis added)

No doubt the reader has noticed that there are two emphasized references to *eight courses/ revolutions*—a clear reference to the orbits of the seven bodies of the solar system tasked by the creator to "distinguish and preserve the numbers of time." Has Timaeus revised his words by declaring now that there are eight bodies to be considered in tracking and measuring time and not seven as he earlier stated? On first appearance, this appears to be the case, and it is not unreasonable to assume that he reversed his earlier decision and decided to add the dwarf planet Ceres to the list. However, a closer reading of the text reveals that the eight courses/revolutions Timaeus refers to here are eight specific measures of time.

Thus then, and for this reason the night and the day were created, being the period of the one most intelligent revolution. And the month is accomplished when the moon has completed her orbit and overtaken the sun, and the year when the sun has completed his own orbit.

Note the reference to "revolution" when Timaeus discusses the time period of day/night in the measure of the day. In this context, he also names and describes two other revolutions, the time periods of the month and year, for a total of three. Note that he describes two revolutions for the Sun, the day and the year, which would not be the case if he were simply naming the revolutions of the heavenly bodies, which revolve in apparent motion about Earth, after them. He would instead name their revolutions once and no more. Unquestionably then, Timaeus is referring to cycles and measures of time when he refers to revolutions and courses, and of the eight revolutions, he names only three. What of the remaining five? He must know them by their revolutions, i.e., time cycles, even if they don't have names, but on this point he is silent as he declines further comment on them.

Mankind, with hardly an exception, have not remarked the periods of the other stars, and they have no name for them, and do not measure them against one another by the help of number, and hence they can scarcely be said to know that their wanderings, being infinite in number and admirable for their variety, make up time. And yet there is no difficulty in seeing that the perfect number of time fulfils the perfect year when all the *eight revolutions* having their relative degrees of swiftness, are accomplished together and attain their completion at the same time, measured by the rotation of the same and equally moving. After this manner, and for these reasons, came into being such of the stars as in their heavenly progress received reversals of motion, to the end that the created heaven might imitate the eternal nature, and be as like as possible to the perfect and intelligible animal. (emphasis added)

Ah, but if Timaeus knows there are eight revolutions, he indeed has more to tell. Humankind may not know them, but he must be an exception, and he does know. However, beyond these few words, he offers nothing. Then again, maybe he does. A close reading of the following text will show that he mentions conjunctions, oppositions, and eclipses, the very stuff of little-known time cycles. Little known that is outside of the circle of astronomers, who do know of them. It is no coincidence that Timaeus is recognized as an astronomer in the opening of Timaeus. (See Critias's words at [27].)

Thus far and until the birth of time the created universe was made in the likeness of the original, but inasmuch as all animals were not yet comprehended therein, it was still unlike. What remained, the creator then proceeded to fashion after the nature of the pattern. Now as in the ideal animal the mind perceives ideas or species of a certain nature and number, he thought that this created animal ought to have species of a like nature and number. There are four such; [40] one of them is the heavenly race of the gods; another, the race of birds whose way is in the air; the third, the watery species; and the fourth, the pedestrian and land creatures. Of the heavenly and divine, he created the greater part out of fire, that they might be the brightest of all things and fairest to behold, and he fashioned them after the likeness of the universe in the figure of a circle, and made them follow the intelligent motion of the supreme, distributing them over the whole circumference of heaven, which was to be a true cosmos or glorious world spangled with them all over. And he gave to each of them two movements: the first, a movement on the same spot after the same manner, whereby they ever continue to think consistently the same thoughts about the same things; the second, a forward movement, in which they are controlled by the revolution of the same and the like; but by the other five motions they were unaffected, in order that each of them might attain the highest perfection. And for this reason the fixed stars were created, to be divine and eternal animals, ever-abiding and revolving after the same manner and on the same spot; and the other stars which reverse their motion and are subject to deviations of this kind, were created in the manner already described. The earth, which is our nurse, clinging around the pole which is extended through the universe, he framed to be the guardian and artificer of night and day, first and eldest of gods that are in the interior of heaven. Vain would be the attempt to tell all the figures of them circling as in dance, and their juxtapositions, and the return of them in their revolutions upon themselves, and their approximations, and to say which of these deities in their conjunctions meet, and which of them are in opposition, and in what order they get behind and before one another, and when they are severally eclipsed to our sight and again reappear, sending terrors and intimations of the future to those who cannot calculate their movements—to attempt to tell of all this without a visible representation of the heavenly system would be labour in vain. Enough on this head; and now let what we have said about the nature of the created and visible gods have an end.

So what are these unnamed five cycles of time? The fourth will be presented and described here and the remaining four in the following chapter.

The fourth revolution of time is the measure of the movement of the Sun and planets in Earth's calendar time as well as the measure of the phenomenon known as the precession of the equinoxes against a background of stars that surround the solar system in a continuous circular band approximately 30 degrees wide. The stars that make up this band of the ecliptic or zodiac in which the Sun and all the planets of the solar system move in their assigned motions with the Sun moving along the center of the band have been known by astronomers for ages.[27] The band of the ecliptic is a part of Timaeus's "revolution of the same." The band(Note in passing. (of the ecliptic permits the locations and movements of the Sun and the planets to be precisely tracked in precise terms of celestial longitude and latitude, or right ascension and declination. These locations are directly associated with Earth's calendar, thus measuring time. Here are Timaeus's words quoted from the foregoing text.

> That there might be some visible measure of their relative swiftness and slowness as they proceeded in their eight course, God lighted a fire, which we now call the sun, in the second from the earth of these orbits, that it might give light to the whole heaven, and the animals [Likely planets of the solar system?] as many as nature intended, *might participate in number, learning arithmetic from the revolution of the same and like.*

> And yet there is no difficulty in seeing that the perfect number of time fulfills the perfect year when all the eight revolutions, having their relative degrees of swiftness, are accomplished together and attain their completion at the same time, *measured by the rotation of the same and equally moving.* (emphasis added)

The sun completes one apparent revolution of the band of the ecliptic each tropical year, the year of the seasons. It is noteworthy that the pattern number, 25,920 [see figure 4, pattern pair (81/32)], is either an exact match or a very close approximation of the length of the Great Year or Platonic year that measures the precession of the equinoxes.

---

[27] Wikipedia, "Ecliptic," Ecliptic - Wikipedia, accessed March 9, 2021.

CHAPTER 7

Revolutions of Time

In the previous chapter, four of the eight revolutions of time mentioned by Timaeus were named and discussed—the day of twenty-four hours, the month of the Moon (likely the synodic month, where the Moon gradually transitions from full Moon to full Moon), the year, where the Sun appears to complete one revolution about Earth and return to the same location against the background stars of the band of the ecliptic on the vernal equinox, and the Great Year as measured by the precession of the equinoxes where the Sun returns to the equinox (specifically at the intersection of the plane of the ecliptic with the plane of the celestial equator) slightly earlier each year in a movement that is measured across the background stars of the band of the ecliptic and is of approximately 25,920 years' duration. The remaining four revolutions of time are not named or described in Timaeus, but there are hints as to their nature found in Timaeus [40], quoted in part below.

> Vain would be the attempt to tell all the figures of them circling as in dance, and their juxtapositions, and the return of them in their revolutions upon themselves, and their approximations, and to say which of these deities in their conjunctions meet, and which of them are in opposition, and in what order they get behind and before one another, and when they are severally eclipsed to our sight and again reappear, sending terrors and intimations of the future to those who cannot calculate their movements.

The first hint is in Timaeus's statement that "Vain would be the attempt to tell all of *the figures of them circling as in dance*, and their juxtapositions, and the return of them in their revolutions upon themselves, and their approximations" (emphasis added).

The figures Timaeus refers to are those derived from the Vesica Pisces figure discussed in chapter 3. It is noteworthy that he also refers to these figures as "circling as in dance," a clear reference to them moving in revolution, i.e., time. What figures? Why the figures generated from the Vesica Pisces, the mother of creation, including the image of the Vesica Pisces itself, which we will begin with? Note from figure 10 below that the two overlapping circles have centers A and B.

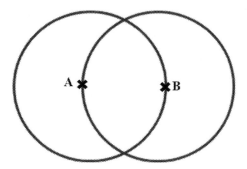

Figure 10
Vesica Pisces

There are several manifestations of time that trace out images of the Vesica Pisces. Two of them are relevant to our discussion.

The first image shows the relationship in time of Earth to the Sun. Point A is the Sun, and it remains stationary but completes an apparent circle each day around Earth, point B, as Earth rotates through 360 degrees on its axis. Meanwhile, with the Sun, point A, stationary, Earth, point B, orbits the Sun and completes a full 360-degree orbit of the Sun each year.

The second image shows the relationship in time of Earth's two poles in the heavens. Point A is the north ecliptic pole, which is pointing at a void in space in the constellation Draco. It is a fixed point, and except for minor movements, it has remined fixed in this position since time began. Point B is the north celestial pole, which is currently pointing at the star Polaris and is the axis around which Earth rotates on its axis 360 degrees each day with point A completing an apparent circle each day around point B. Meanwhile, point B is also slowly orbiting through a full circle around point A in a 25,920-year period with point A remaining stationary. This latter movement is another manifestation of the precession of the equinoxes.

The time revolutions that derive directly from the Vesica Pisces are the day, the year, and the Great Year. The two examples of the Vesica Pisces discussed above do not describe those additional time revolutions that derive from the figures or shapes, which derive from the Vesica Pisces—an important distinction.

a. The Shapes of Time

Three shapes derived from the Vesica Pisces were detailed in chapter 3.

1. The circle within a circle (see [36], which states, "and comprehending them in a uniform revolution upon the same axis, he made one the outer and the other the inner circle.")

2. The equilateral triangle, which is formed by the bisected almond-shape of the Vesica Pisces (see figure 6 in chapter 3).

3. The five-pointed star shape that arises from the icosahedron (see chapter 1, specifically figure 3, and chapter 3).

In astronomical terms, the circle in a circle would manifest itself as any of three types of conjunctions where two heavenly bodies also overlap one another.

1. the eclipse where bodies of the same or approximately the same size overlap,

2. the transit, where a smaller body passes in front of a larger one, or

3. the occultation, where a larger body passes in front of and occults a smaller one.

The equilateral triangle and five-pointed star are patterns formed by the periodic and predictable movements of specific bodies. These three figures are shown below.

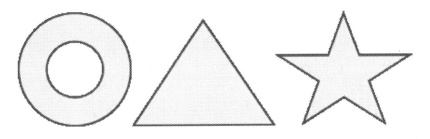

Figure 11
The three figures that manifest themselves in the solar system

Each of these three patterns is associated with one or more time revolutions as follows. They are numbered 5 through 8, and together, they constitute the remaining four, time revolutions not named by Timaeus. It should be noted that the Moon and the planets in their respective movements create many conjunctions, eclipses, transits, and occultations other than those listed below. Aside from the fact that the four listed here are manifestations of these three figures, they are also the best known and the most widely followed in astronomical circles. Several others are also mentioned and described, but they are <u>not</u> numbered.

Revolutions of Time Deriving from the Circle in a Circle

5. The Saros Eclipse Cycle

The saros eclipse cycle is the most accurate and reliable cycle for predicting solar and lunar eclipses. Within a specific series (there are approximately forty-two of them at any given period of time), there are some seventy-two separate eclipse members over the 1,296-year life of the series each separated by an 18.03-year period of time.[28] (See entry for the Exeligmos Eclipse Cycle under, Time Cycles Deriving from the Equilateral Triangle, following.)

6. The Venus Transit Cycle

Venus transits the Sun three or four times in a 243-year long cycle. These transits are grouped together by related members in a series that persists for long periods. Venus transit series are analogous to saros eclipse series.[29]

Revolutions of Time Deriving from the Equilateral Triangle

7. Jupiter/Saturn Conjunctions

Jupiter conjuncts, i.e., appears in the same celestial longitude with Saturn once every twenty years on average. Three successive Jupiter/Saturn conjunctions define an equilateral triangle. This time revolution is called the Great Conjunction.[30]

____The Exeligmos Eclipse Cycle.

In the exeligmos eclipse cycle, any three successive eclipse members of a saros series, while each are separated by a period of 18.03 years, are also offset geographically by an approximately 120-degree westward movement in latitude from one another. The third successive member completes the exeligmos cycle, which will take place in approximately the same location as the first one, some 54.1 years later, thus completing a 360-degree circle, with its three saros eclipse cycle members describing an equilateral triangle. The equilateral triangular pattern described by the exeligmos eclipse cycle is not considered to be a separate time revolution for measuring time; rather, for the instant purposes, it is considered to be an aspect of the saros eclipse cycle so as to not count the saros cycle twice.

Revolutions of Time Deriving from the Five-Pointed Star

8. Venus Inferior Conjunctions

Venus arrives at inferior conjunction with Earth, i.e., between Earth and the Sun on the same celestial longitude, once every 584 days or 19.8 months. There is a synchronicity in these conjunctions with five conjunctions occurring in eight Earth years and in thirteen Venus years of 225 days each. These three numbers—5, 8, 13—are three successive numbers of the Fibonacci

---

[28] NASA Eclipse Web Site, "Eclipses and the Saros" Fred Espenak, NASA - Eclipses and the Saros. accessed November 11, 2021

[29] NASA Catalogue of Six Millennium Catalogue of Venus Transits—2,000 BCE to 4,000 CE, NASA - Catalog of Transits of Venus. accessed November 11, 2021

[30] Wikipedia, "Great conjunction," Great conjunction - Wikipedia, accessed March 11, 2021.

series, which are related to one another by the golden ratio. Five successive Venus inferior conjunctions define the five-pointed star.[31]

___Venus/Moon Conjunctions

After Venus appears as an evening star and then is no longer visible in the heavens, it reappears as a morning star some eight days later. During the eight-day period when Venus is not visible, it passes through inferior conjunction with Earth and the Sun. A crescent moon appears with Venus in a truly spectacular display in the heavens once every 584 days, 19.8 months, first when Venus is an evening star and then when it is a morning star. However, the 584-day cycle applies only to sequential Venus appearances as an evening or a morning star. In other words, if a crescent moon appears in conjunction with Venus as an evening star, a similar conjunction will appear 584 days later. Also, if a crescent moon appears with Venus as an evening or morning star, a conjunction of the two will appear again almost on the same date eight years later; this latter cycle is called the octaeteris cycle. There are five Venus-Moon conjunctions each separated by 584 days in an octaeteris cycle, thus tracing out the five-pointed star pattern. This pattern does not constitute a separate time revolution as its cycle is identical to that of the pattern of the Venus inferior conjunction cycle, and is considered to be an aspect of this same cycle.[32]

There is one remaining issue to be addressed—Timaeus's statement that the eight revolutions complete a perfect number of time when their motions are accomplished together.

> And yet there is no difficulty in seeing that the perfect number of time fulfils the perfect year when all the eight revolutions, having their relative degrees of swiftness, are accomplished together and attain their completion at the same time, measured by the rotation of the same and equally moving.

Is there such a number? Yes, it is 77,760 years, which can be divided by the period of time for each of the eight specific time revolutions mentioned.

1. The day of twenty-four hours.
2. The lunar synodic month of 29.5 days each, twelve in a lunar year. (Although the nature of the lunar month is not specified, Timaeus states that the month "is accomplished when the moon has completed her orbit and overtaken the sun," which describes the synodic month, not the sidereal month.)

---

[31] Wikipedia, "Venus," Venus - Wikipedia, accessed March 11, 2021. See section 3.3, "Pentagram of Venus" under 3, Observability.

[32] Wikipedia, "Octaeteris," Octaeteris - Wikipedia, accessed March 11, 2021.

3. The tropical year of 365.24 days.
4. The Great Year of the precession of the eclipses, 25,920 years.
5. The duration of a saros eclipse series, 1,296 years.
6. The duration of a Venus transit cycle, 243 years.
7. The duration of a Great Conjunction cycle of Jupiter and Saturn, 20 years.
8. The duration of a Venus inferior conjunction cycle, 8 years.

The first two—the day and the lunar synodic month—are accomplished multiple times each year, and the tropical year is accomplished once each year, so all three complete the perfect number of 77,760 years. The remaining five are each integers of the perfect number. It is noteworthy that all these numbers including the duration numbers from the time revolutions, the perfect number as well as the factors, are numbers from the pattern.

1. There are three Great Years of 25,920 years duration each in 77,760.
2. There are sixty saros series durations of 1,296 years each in 77,760.
3. There are 320 Venus transit series durations of 243 years each in 77,760.
4. There are 3,888 Great Conjunction cycles of twenty years' duration each in 77,760.
5. There are 9,720 Venus inferior conjunction cycles of eight years' duration each in 77,760.

The perfect number will repeat every 77,760 years.
From form and motion, then, God brought forth number and created time.

b. Atlantis and the Periodic Destruction of Earth

Readers who have read the appended sections of Timaeus from start to finish will have undoubtedly noticed that they begin with a brief discussion of the destruction of Atlantis, a tale that Plato takes up in much greater detail in Critias. I will not delve into this topic except to briefly point out that it contains several important clues as to the nature of the catastrophe that befell not only Atlantis but the whole of Earth. From [22].

> Thereupon one of the priests, who was of a very great age, said: O Solon, Solon, you Hellenes are never anything but children, and there is not an old man among you. Solon in return asked him what he meant. I mean to say, he replied, that in mind you are all young; there is no old opinion handed down among you by ancient tradition, nor any science which is hoary with age. And I will tell you why. There have been, and will be again, many destructions of mankind arising out of many causes; the greatest have been brought about by the agencies of fire and water, and other lesser ones by innumerable other causes. There is a story,

which even you have preserved, that once upon a time Paethon, the son of Helios, having yoked the steeds in his father's chariot, because he was not able to drive them in the path of his father, burnt up all that was upon the earth, and was himself destroyed by a thunderbolt. *Now this has the form of a myth, but really signifies a declination of the bodies moving in the heavens around the earth, and a great conflagration of things upon the earth, which recurs after long intervals*; at such times those who live upon the mountains and in dry and lofty places are more liable to destruction than those who dwell by rivers or on the seashore. And from this calamity the Nile, who is our never-failing saviour, delivers and preserves us. When, on the other hand, the gods purge the earth with a deluge of water, the survivors in your country are herdsmen and shepherds who dwell on the mountains, but those who, like you, live in cities are carried by the rivers into the sea. Whereas in this land, neither then nor at any other time, does the water come down from above on the fields, having always a tendency to come up from below; for which reason the traditions preserved here are the most ancient.

The fact is, that wherever the extremity of winter frost or of summer does not prevent, mankind exist, sometimes in greater, [23] sometimes in lesser numbers. And whatever happened either in your country or in ours, or in any other region of which we are informed—if there were any actions noble or great or in any other way remarkable, they have all been written down by us of old, and are preserved in our temples. Whereas just when you and other nations are beginning to be provided with letters and the other requisites of civilized life, after the usual interval, the stream from heaven, like a pestilence, comes pouring down, and leaves only those of you who are destitute of letters and education; and so you have to begin all over again like children, and know nothing of what happened in ancient times, either among us or among yourselves. As for those genealogies of yours which you just now recounted to us, Solon, they are no better than the tales of children. In the first place you remember a single deluge only, but there were many previous ones; in the next place, you do not know that there formerly dwelt in your land the fairest and noblest race of men which ever lived, and that you and your whole city are descended from a small seed or remnant of them which survived. And this was unknown to you, because, for many generations, the survivors of that destruction died, leaving no written word. For there was a time, Solon, before the great deluge of all, when the city which now is Athens was first in war and in every way the best governed of all cities, is said to have performed

42

the noblest deeds and to have had the fairest constitution of any of which tradition tells, under the face of heaven. (emphasis added)

The emphasized text clearly points to the cause of the catastrophe as "a declination of bodies moving in the heavens around the earth." This formulation uses a geocentric perspective of the event signifying that time was involved and that the event involved planets and their declination, a form of celestial latitude. Planets conjunct one another quite frequently in their motions when they reach the same celestial longitude, but they occult one another much less frequently when they reach the same declination or celestial latitude. And some occultations such as that of Saturn by Jupiter are extremely rare events occurring only once every 4,000 or more years.[33] Could an occultation of Saturn by Jupiter be the proximate cause of these catastrophes that periodically befall Earth? I will say nothing further in this regard here as it would prove too great of a distraction from this book's purposes, but there is a far larger tale to be told.

---

[33] Wikipedia, "Occultation," Occultation - Wikipedia, accessed May 6, 2021.

CHAPTER 8

Space—The Vessel of the Universe

That there is space in which the created universe exists may seem to be such an obvious and sensible aspect of creation that it should bear little mention and need no discussion. And yet Timaeus devotes considerable narrative to it and considers it so important that he offers up a prayer again to God for guidance in discussing it as he did at the very beginning of his story of creation.

Along with the eternal pattern of creation and the moving image of it that is made manifest as time, he considers space the third essential aspect of creation. In many respects, this is the easiest of the many subjects Timaeus covers to present and discuss, but in a very fundamental way, it is the most difficult of all to fully comprehend. Perhaps that is why even Timaeus struggles to fully explain it, which is why I will let him tell the tale in his own words as I cannot offer any further comment on or clarification of the subject. Timaeus proceeds.

Once more, then, at the commencement of my discourse, I call upon God, and beg him to be our saviour out of a strange and unwonted enquiry, and to bring us to the haven of probability. So now let us begin again.

This new beginning of our discussion of the universe requires a fuller division than the former; for then we made two classes, now a third must be revealed. The two sufficed for the former discussion: one, which we assumed, was a pattern intelligible and always the same; [49] and the second was only the imitation of the pattern, generated and visible. There is also a third kind which we did not distinguish at the time, conceiving that the two would be enough. But now the argument seems to require that we should set forth in words another kind, which is difficult of explanation and dimly seen. What nature are we to attribute to this new kind of being? We reply, that it is the receptacle, and in a manner the nurse, of all generation. I have spoken the truth; but I must express myself in clearer language, and this will be an arduous task for many reasons, and in particular because I must first raise questions concerning fire and the other elements, and determine what each of them is; for to say, with any probability or certitude, which of them should be called water rather than fire, and which should be called any of them rather than all or some one of them, is a difficult matter. How, then, shall we settle this point, and what questions about the elements may be fairly raised?

But as Timaeus further explains, space is not mere emptiness but an invisible and formless matrix in which the universe is brought forth by the creator and the invisible and formless being in which it continues its existence thereafter.

But the forms which enter into and go out of her are the likenesses of real existences modelled after their patterns in wonderful and inexplicable manner, which we will hereafter investigate. For the present we have only to conceive of three natures: first, that which is in process of generation; secondly, that in which the generation takes place; and thirdly, that of which the thing generated is a resemblance. And we may liken the receiving principle to a mother, and the source or spring to a father, and the intermediate nature to a child; and may remark further, that if the model is to take every variety of form, then the matter in which the model is fashioned will not be duly prepared, unless it is formless, and free from the impress of any of these shapes which it is hereafter to receive from without. For if the matter were like any of the supervening forms, then whenever any opposite or entirely different nature was stamped upon its surface, it would take the impression badly, because it would intrude its own shape. Wherefore, that which is to receive all forms should have no form; as in making perfumes they first contrive that the liquid substance which is to receive the scent shall be as inodorous as possible; or as those who wish to impress figures on soft substances do not allow any previous impression to remain, [51] but begin by making the surface as even and smooth as possible. In the same way that which is to receive perpetually and through its whole extent the resemblances of all eternal beings ought to be devoid of any particular form. Wherefore, the mother and receptacle of all created and visible and in any way sensible things, is not to be termed earth, or air, or fire, or water, or any of their compounds or any of the elements from which these are derived, but is an invisible and formless being which receives all things and in some mysterious way partakes of the intelligible, and is most incomprehensible. In saying this we shall not be far wrong; as far, however, as we can attain to a knowledge of her from the previous considerations, we may truly say that fire is that part of her nature which from time to time is inflamed, and water that which is moistened, and that the mother substance becomes earth and air, in so far as she receives the impressions of them.

Of particular note from the foregoing passage is Timaeus's concluding statement that space "is an invisible and formless being, which receives all things and in some mysterious way partakes of the intelligible, and is most incomprehensible." Space "partakes of the intelligible"? I can offer no comment on that point.

Timaeus concludes,

> Thus I state my view:—If mind and true opinion are two distinct classes, then I say that there certainly are these self-existent ideas unperceived by sense, and apprehended only by the mind; if, however, as some say, true opinion differs in no respect from mind, then everything that we perceive through the body is to be regarded as most real and certain. But we must affirm that to be distinct, for they have a distinct origin and are of a different nature; the one is implanted in us by instruction, the other by persuasion; the one is always accompanied by true reason, the other is without reason; the one cannot be overcome by persuasion, but the other can: and lastly, every man may be said to share in true opinion, but mind is the attribute of the gods and of very few men. Wherefore also we must acknowledge that there is one kind of being which is always the same, [52] uncreated and indestructible, never receiving anything into itself from without, nor itself going out to any other, but invisible and imperceptible by any sense, and of which the contemplation is granted to intelligence only. And there is another nature of the same name with it, and like to it, perceived by sense, created, always in motion, becoming in place and again vanishing out of place, which is apprehended by opinion and sense. And there is a third nature, which is space, and is eternal, and admits not of destruction and provides a home for all created things, and is apprehended without the help of sense, by a kind of spurious reason, and is hardly real; which we beholding as in a dream, say of all existence that it must of necessity be in some place and occupy a space, but that what is neither in heaven nor in earth has no existence. Of these and other things of the same kind, relating to the true and waking reality of nature, we have only this dreamlike sense, and we are unable to cast off sleep and determine the truth about them. For an image, since the reality, after which it is modelled, does not belong to it, and it exists ever as the fleeting shadow of some other, must be inferred to be in another [i.e. in space], grasping existence in some way or other, or it could not be

at all. But true and exact reason, vindicating the nature of true being, maintains that while two things [i.e. the image and space] are different they cannot exist one of them in the other and so be one and also two at the same time.

I apologize that I cannot offer anything further on this subject, only the observation that Timaeus regards it of the utmost importance. In this regard he is certainly correct, for if there were no space, creation could not have happened and the universe could not exist. To paraphrase Timaeus, perhaps it will always be mysterious to us and ultimately not fully knowable, something we can attain only a certain dreamlike comprehension of.

CHAPTER 9

Soul and Energy

Timaeus clearly states throughout his narrative that fire is one of the four elements of creation. In current times, fire is understood to be a visible manifestation of energy that can be observed throughout the universe, and it is further understood by science that besides fire, there are manifestations of many other forms of energy including, electromagnetic, gravity, nuclear, etc., Some are visible though most are not.

In Timaeus, aside from fire, there is no specific mention of energy in any form. However, Timaeus makes frequent reference to the soul, one of the two elements of creation—soul and matter (earth, wind, fire, and water)—from which a third, essence, was synthesized. Timaeus states that the soul is the primal element of all creation, which was placed at the center of creation, that it permeates all aspect of the visible universe, and that it acts as a surrounding environment for the universe. In current times, science has little to say about soul or the concept of one or that there could be such an element in the universe. Timaeus had no such doubts. To him, soul is self-evident throughout the universe though invisible and formless.

So are Timaeus's concepts of soul and its manifestation throughout the universe just antiquated understandings or the products of a belief system long since repudiated as modern science seems to widely believe because such concepts lack any form of verifiable proof? Or is there a misunderstanding of Timaeus's concept of soul in modern science? I believe it is the latter, a misunderstanding. While Timaeus's understanding of soul is foreign and illogical to modern science, if he is using the concept to refer to energy, much of what he says of soul makes perfect sense. It is probably no coincidence then that while modern science recognizes that the universe is composed of the basic elements of energy and mass, Timaeus long ago may have referred to these same elements as soul and matter. The questions to be considered then if Timaeus's concept of a universal soul is accurate are, Could soul manifest itself as energy, which is also invisible and formless, and present throughout the universe? Or are energy and soul simply one and the same and their terms merely synonymous?

One of the most famous equations in scientific history, Einstein's $E = mc^2$, derives from the fact that energy and mass are interchangeable, a concept that may have intrigued Timaeus if he were alive today to consider it. However, Timaeus maintained that their equivalents in his estimation, soul and matter, were separate elements and not interchangeable; instead, they were combined with one another and present throughout all creation. Is this a minor disagreement or a fundamental difference of opinion? Probably a minor disagreement as modern science also subscribes to a proposition called the conservation of energy,[34] which holds that energy cannot be destroyed in an isolated environment. According to Timaeus, soul not only permeates the universe; it also provides "the exterior environment of it" (see [34] below). Soul, then, is finite and exists in a limited environment or isolation. This topic could well prove an interesting discussion, but it is premature and a distraction at this point. After all, it has merely been hypothesized—not proven—that soul is synonymous with energy in Timaeus. We will have to closely exam Timaeus's words in speaking of soul to proceed further with such a hypothesis.

Unfortunately, Timaeus does not speak at any great length about the nature of soul, but what he does say is intriguing. He states that soul is intelligent and present in *all* creation. This would seem to affirm that both gravity and electromagnetic energy are intelligible presences in the universe (recall that soul and matter were combined and synthesized into measure and number) as both have dimension and can be measured. But is this the same thing as their being shaped and formed by a universal element of creation, the soul? No, it is not, but there is more in Timaeus on this point. Consider that soul was created by God and why he created it.

Let me tell you then why the creator made this world of generation. He was good, and the good can never have any jealousy of anything. And being free from jealousy, he desired that all things should be as like himself as they could be. This is in the truest sense the origin of creation and of the world, [30] as we shall do well in believing on the testimony of wise men: God desired that all things should be good and nothing bad, so far as this was attainable. Wherefore also finding the whole visible sphere not at rest, but moving in an irregular and disorderly fashion, out of disorder he brought order, considering that this was in every way better than the other. Now the deeds of the best could never be or have been other than the fairest; and the creator, reflecting on the things which are by nature visible, found that no unintelligent creature taken as a whole was fairer than the intelligent taken as a whole; and that intelligence could not be present in anything which was devoid of soul. *For which reason, when he was framing the universe, he put intelligence in soul, and soul in body, that he might be the creator of a work which was by nature fairest and best. Wherefore, using the language of*

---

[34] Wikipedia, "Conservation of Energy," Conservation of energy - Wikipedia, accessed March 18, 2021.

probability, we may say that the world became a living creature truly endowed with
soul and intelligence by the providence of God. (emphasis added)

He describes soul as older than and the ruler and mistress of the body at [34–35].

Such was the whole plan of the eternal God about the god that was to be, to whom for this reason he gave a body, smooth and even, having a surface in every direction equidistant from the centre, a body entire and perfect, and formed out of perfect bodies. *And in the centre he put the soul, which he diffused throughout the body, making it also to be the exterior environment of it*; and he made the universe a circle moving in a circle, one and solitary, yet by reason of its excellence able to converse with itself, and needing no other friendship or acquaintance. Having these purposes in view he created the world a blessed god.

Now God did not make the soul after the body, although we are speaking of them in this order; for having brought them together he would never have allowed that the elder should be ruled by the younger; but this is a random manner of speaking which we have, because somehow we ourselves too are very much under the dominion of chance. *Whereas he made the soul in origin and excellence prior to and older than the body, to be the ruler and mistress, of whom the body was to be the subject.* (emphasis added)

An important question to consider at this point: If fire is a manifestation of energy, does this not negate any possibility of energy being either soul or synonymous with soul? Fire is quite clearly energy, and the light it gives off is part of the visible component of the electromagnetic spectrum of radiant energy, and as Timaeus definitively states that fire is one of the four material components of creation, this would seem to eliminate any possibility of there being a connection between soul and energy.

However, there is more to consider. While fire is energy, fire is also matter according to Timaeus, and as such, it was shaped and ordered by the action of the prior existing, more authoritative, and controlling hand of soul as can be learned from [34] as cited above: "Whereas he made the soul in origin and excellence prior to and older than the body, to be the ruler and mistress, of whom the body was to be the subject." So according to Timaeus, fire, as a part of the material body of creation, was shaped and formed by soul, and as such, fire may be that aspect of the soul as energy that soul shares with matter. Thus, fire is both energy and material.

This finding is consistent with modern science, which states that fire is the rapid oxidation of combustible material.[35] The flames are the visible aspect of this process.

Timaeus speaks again of soul at [37].

> Now when the Creator had framed the soul according to his will, he formed within her the corporeal universe *The soul, interfused everywhere from the centre to the circumference of heaven, of which also she is the external envelopment*, and brought the two together, and united them centre to centre. herself turning in herself, began a divine beginning of never ceasing and rational life enduring throughout all time. [37] The body of heaven is visible, but the soul is invisible, and partakes of reason and harmony, and being made by the best of intellectual and everlasting natures, is the best of things created. And because she is composed of the same and of the other and of the essence, these three, and is divided and united in due proportion, and in her revolutions returns upon herself, *the soul, when touching anything which has essence, whether dispersed in parts or undivided, is stirred through all her powers, to declare the sameness or difference of that thing and some other; and to what individuals are related, and by what affected, and in what way and how and when, both in the world of generation and in the world of immutable being.* And when reason, which works with equal truth, whether she be in the circle of the diverse or of the same—in voiceless silence holding her onward course in the sphere of the self-moved—when reason, I say, is hovering around the sensible world and when the circle of the diverse also moving truly imparts the intimations of sense to the whole soul, then arise opinions and beliefs sure and certain. But when reason is concerned with the rational, and the circle of the same moving smoothly declares it, then intelligence and knowledge are necessarily perfected. And if anyone affirms that in which these two are found to be other than the soul, he will say the very opposite of the truth. (emphasis added)

Energy can be measured and is intelligible, attributes it holds in common with soul. The concept of charge in electromagnetic terms can basically be defined as like attracts opposite and like repels like, which sounds similar to an attribute of soul in Timaeus.

> The soul, when touching anything which has essence, whether dispersed in parts or undivided, is stirred through all her powers, to declare the sameness or difference of that thing and some other, and to what individuals are related,

---

[35] Wikipedia, "Fire," https://en.wikipedia.org/wiki/Fire accessed March 19, 2021.

and by what affected, and in what way and how and when, both in the world of generation and in the world of immutable being. (See emphasized text in foregoing citation.)

And from [45], perhaps the most telling passage of all.

> And so in the vessel of the head, they first of all put a face in which they inserted organs to minister in all things to the providence of the soul, and they appointed this part, which has authority, to be by nature the part which is in front. And of the organs they first contrived the eyes to give light, and the principle according to which they were inserted was as follows: So much of fire as would not burn, but gave a gentle light, they formed into a substance akin to the light of every-day life; *and the pure fire which is within us and related thereto* they made to flow through the eyes in a stream smooth and dense, compressing the whole eye, and especially the centre part, so that it kept out everything of a coarser nature, and allowed to pass only this pure element. (emphasis added)

In this short excerpt, it is clearly stated that there is a difference between fire and light. Fire burns whereas light is of a different nature—one that is related to the pure fire or light of the soul. A close reading of the text cited above strongly suggests that Timaeus understands that light and soul are synonymous. And since modern science indisputably understands that light is energy, the term *soul* to Timaeus means energy, specifically radiant energy or its manifestation. Furthermore, since Timaeus states that soul is pervasive throughout the universe and does not mention different categories of soul, the soul of the universe must be of the same nature as that of humankind.

There is nothing further of substance on this issue from Timaeus to consider. Is this enough then to answer our earlier questions: Could soul manifest itself as energy? Or are energy and soul simply one and the same and their terms merely synonymous? I am being as objective as I can about this issue when I say that there is not sufficient evidence at hand to answer either question with certainty. I cast about Timaeus for the number and geometry that provided such firm ground on which to proceed as earlier, but there is seemingly none to be found. Or is there? The five-pointed star of the icosahedron and radiant energy in the form of electromagnetic energy and gravity,[36] both of which permeate the universe, may provide clues. However, there is another matter that must be addressed first.

---

[36] Wikipedia, "Radiant Energy," Radiant energy - Wikipedia, accessed March 20, 2021.

CHAPTER 10

Harmony and the Proportions of Matter— Earth, Wind, Fire, and Water

This may be a subject that should have been addressed earlier, but it is such an enigmatic subject written in such cryptic terms that I deferred delving into it until now.

Now that which is created is of necessity corporeal, and also visible and tangible. And nothing is visible where there is no fire, or tangible which has no solidity, and nothing is solid without earth. Wherefore also God in the beginning of creation made the body of the universe to consist of fire and earth. But two things cannot be rightly put together without a third; there must be some bond of union between them. *And the fairest bond is that which makes the most complete fusion of itself and the things which it combines; and proportion is best adapted to effect such a union.* For whenever in any three numbers, whether cube or square, there is a mean, which is to the last term what the first term is to it; [32] and again, when the mean is to the first term as the last term is to the mean—then the mean becoming first and last, and the first and last both becoming means, they will all of them of necessity come to be the same, and having become the same with one another will be all one. If the universal frame had been created a surface only and having no depth, a single mean would have sufficed to bind together itself and the other terms; but now, as the world must be solid, and solid bodies are always compacted not by one mean but by two, *God placed water and air in the mean between fire and earth, and made them to have the same proportion so far as was possible (as fire is to air so is air to water, and as air is to water so is water to earth)*; and thus he bound and put together a visible and tangible heaven. And for these reasons, and out of such elements which are in number four, the body of the world was created, and it was harmonised by proportion, and therefore has the spirit of friendship; and

53

having been reconciled to itself, it was indissoluble by the hand of any other than the framer. (emphasis added)

The sequence with which the shapes were introduced by Timaeus at [55]—tetrahedron, octahedron, icosahedron, and cube—used in conjunction with the sequence of the listing of the elements from the foregoing at [32] and from the sequence at [56] as cited below, was used to associate the shapes with the elements.

> *To earth, then, let us assign the cubical form;* for earth is the most immoveable of the four and the most plastic of all bodies, and that which has the most stable bases must of necessity be of such a nature. Now, of the triangles which we assumed at first, that which has two equal sides is by nature more firmly based than that which has unequal sides; and of the compound figures which are formed out of either, the plane equilateral quadrangle has necessarily, a more stable basis than the equilateral triangle, both in the whole and in the parts. [56] Wherefore, in assigning this figure to earth, we adhere to probability; and to water we assign that one of the remaining forms which is the least moveable; and the most moveable of them to fire; and to air that which is intermediate. Also we assign the smallest body to fire, and the greatest to water, and the intermediate in size to air; and, again, the acutest body to fire, and the next in acuteness to, air, and the third to water. Of all these elements, that which has the fewest bases must necessarily be the most moveable, for it must be the acutest and most penetrating in every way, and also the lightest as being composed of the smallest number of similar particles: and the second body has similar properties in a second degree, and the third body in the third degree. *Let it be agreed, then, both according to strict reason and according to probability, that the pyramid is the solid which is the original element and seed of fire; and let us assign the element which was next in the order of generation to air, and the third to water.* We must imagine all these to be so small that no single particle of any of the four kinds is seen by us on account of their smallness: but when many of them are collected together their aggregates are seen. And the ratios of their numbers, motions, and other properties, everywhere God, as far as necessity allowed or gave consent, has exactly perfected, and harmonised in due proportion. (emphasis added)

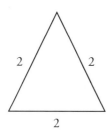 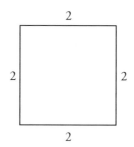

Figure 12

Equilateral triangle and square

Given the dimensions of the two shapes in figure 12, their respective areas are these.

Equilateral triangle: height $\sqrt{3}$ ½ base of 2 = ½ · 2 · $\sqrt{3}$ = 1 · $\sqrt{3}$ = $\sqrt{3}$

Square 2 · 2 = 4

The four Platonic solids mentioned by Timaeus at [55] and their associated element as noted at [32] in parentheses as well as the number of faces and the shape that each face has are these.

1. Tetrahedron (fire)—4 equilateral triangular faces
2. Octahedron (wind)—8 equilateral triangular faces
3. Icosahedron (water)—20 equilateral triangular faces
4. Cube (earth)—6 square faces

While Timaeus speaks of solids, he describes them solely by their exterior surfaces never mentioning the interior aspects or measures of any of them and specifically their volumetric measures. This is not a problematic omission as the missing dimensions can readily be determined. However, it does suggest that his focus was exclusively on these surface dimensions as will ours for the moment.

The surface area of each of the shapes described earlier is as follows (number of faces · area of each face):

1. Tetrahedron (fire)—4 · $\sqrt{3}$ = 6.928
2. Octahedron (wind)—8 · $\sqrt{3}$ = 13.856
3. Icosahedron (water)—20 · $\sqrt{3}$ = 34.64
4. Cube (earth)—6 · 4 = 24

Their proportional relationships are: fire (6.928), wind (13.856), water (34.64), and earth (24). Based on their proportional relationships, their means as Timaeus calls them are the following.

- Fire (6.928) : Wind (13.856)—their mean is 2 (6.928 · 2 = 13.856)
- Wind (13.856) : Water (34.64)—their mean is 2.5 (13.856 · 2.5 = 34.64)
- Water (34.64) : Earth (24)—their mean is .6928 (34.64 · .6928 = 24; note that .6928 is the first term, fire, (6.928/10 = .6928.)

Additionally, there are several other means that can be derived. :

- Fire (6.928) : Earth (24)—their mean is 3.464 (6.928 · 3.464 = 24; note that 3.464 is the third term, water, or 34.64/10 = 3.464)
- Fire (6.928) : Water (34.64)—their mean is 5 (6.928 · 5 = 34.64)
- Wind (13.856) : Earth (24)—their mean is 1.732 (13.856 · 1.732 = 24; note that 1.732 is the $\sqrt{3}$, which is the area of the equilateral triangle in our argument here.)

These means and their relationships to the elements are confirmed in Timaeus [57].

From all that we have just been saying about the elements or kinds, the most probable conclusion is as follows: earth, when meeting with fire and dissolved by its sharpness, whether the dissolution take place in the fire itself or perhaps in some mass of air or water, is borne hither and thither, until its parts, meeting together and mutually harmonizing, again become earth; for they can never take any other form. But water, when divided by fire or by air, on reforming, may become one part fire and two parts ai ; and a single volume of air divided becomes two of fire. Again, when a small body of fire is contained in a larger body of air or water or earth, and both are moving, and the fire struggling is overcome and broken up, then two volumes of fire form one volume of air; and when air is overcome and cut up into small pieces, two and a half parts of air are condensed into one part of water. Let us consider the matter in another way. When one of the other elements is fastened upon by fire, [57] and is cut by the sharpness of its angles and sides, it coalesces with the fire, and then ceases to be cut by them any longer.

If we plot these terms and their means on an equilateral triangle that has had three additional line segments added to it each of which bisects an interior angle of the triangle and meets at the center of the triangle, their relationships can more readily be seen. Interestingly, if this image is also shaded, it has a 3D aspect to it viewed from the bottom up; in other words, it's a solid. More to the point, it is a tetrahedron, the first Platonic solid—which is how Timaeus described the arrangement of the terms and means. (See figure 13 following.)

Recall that 6.928, which appears at the center of the triangle, is the element fire; 13.586, which appears at the right point of the triangle, is the element air; 34.64, which appears at the left point of the triangle, is water; and finally, 24, which appears at the apex point of the triangle, is the element earth. While I have arranged these four numbers (elements) in this particular manner, there is no reason that it could not have been done so in a different manner, for instance, with earth in the center and the other three elements located at each of the three points of the triangle. The only requirement is that the order of the means between them must be exact. Note that any three terms or elements—the bolded and underlined numbers—have two different means, one between each two elements.

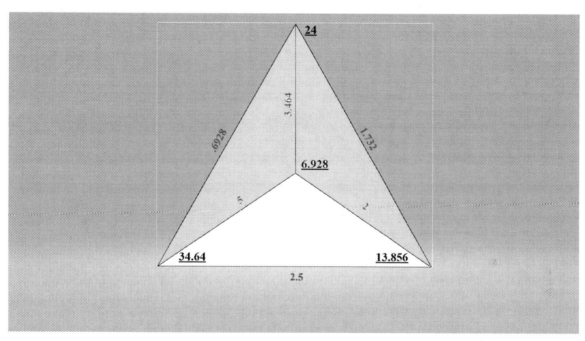

Figure 13

Equilateral triangle with terms (elements) and means plotted

Two things can be gleaned from this figure. The first is that the text of Timaeus cited earlier describing the terms and their means and the changing order of their appearance can more readily be understood.

> For whenever in any three numbers, whether cube or square, there is a mean, which is to the last term what the first term is to it; [32] and again, when the mean is to the first term as the last term is to the mean—then the mean becoming first and last, and the first and last both becoming means, they will all of them of necessity come to be the same, and having become the same with one another will be all one. *If the universal frame had been created a surface only and having no*

> *depth, a single mean would have sufficed to bind together itself and the other terms;*
> *but now, as the world must be solid, and solid bodies are always compacted not by*
> *one mean but by two.* (emphasis added)

Also, the interchangeable nature of the terms and means can more readily be grasped. Choose any three means in sequence and there are three terms—elements— between them.

And second, the expression "will be all one" is more easily understood.

Are these terms and means not all part of the same proportions? And because the terms (elements) do not have to be arranged in any particular order, are they not also "all one"?

All the numbers cited here whether terms or their bonds are derived from forms or variations of two and three.

$$6.928 = \sqrt{3} \cdot 2^2$$
$$.6928 = \sqrt{3} \cdot 2/10$$
$$34.64 = \sqrt{3} \cdot 20$$
$$3.464 = \sqrt{3} \cdot 2$$
$$2.5 = 1/.2 \cdot \tfrac{1}{2}$$
$$13.856 = \sqrt{3} \cdot 2^3$$
$$24 = 3 \cdot 2^3$$
$$2 = 2$$
$$5 = 1/.2$$
$$\sqrt{3} = \sqrt{3}$$

Are two and three the two means of solid bodies that Timaeus refers to in the earlier quote? It is certainly possible.

There is another possibility, as well, one that directly deals with the issue of solid bodies. (See the emphasized text in the foregoing quotation from Timaeus.) This text clearly states that solid bodies require two means, but are there only two, or are there more as argued earlier? If only two, what are they? The ensuing section [33] of Timaeus deals with the shape of the world and states that it is a sphere or globe.

> Wherefore he made the world in the form of a globe, round as from a lathe, having
> its extremes in every direction equidistant from the centre, the most perfect and
> the most like itself of all figures; for he considered that the like is infinitely fairer
> than the unlike.

If we are dealing with a globe or sphere, a form that all the Platonic solids comprehend within their shapes, the issue of radius and circumference must be addressed. (It is particularly noteworthy that Timaeus's words in the foregoing quote quite clearly contemplate the radius of a globe.) One of them is particularly relevant to our argument—the radius or midradius of the midsphere—the sphere that is tangent at the midpoint of each edge—of the icosahedron, which is phi or the golden ratio.[37] Here we are back at the very beginning of this book, in chapter 1, where the radius of Earth was determined to be the product of phi or 1.618034 and the $\sqrt{3}$ or 1.7320508 and the $\sqrt{2}$ or 1.4142135. From this product, 3.9633576589, the measure of Earth's radius and circumference were derived as well as the measure of pi, 3.141640786 (see chapter 1.) So are phi and pi the two means contemplated by Timaeus? It is a distinct possibility. However, this begs the question as to which means, the ones earlier described, or phi and pi, the ones contemplated by Timaeus? In my opinion, both sets are likely as both sets appear to be essential to the creation of Earth. The ramifications of this are staggering and involve all four elements found in Earth's creation in harmonious unity just as Timaeus said.

Continuing in this vein, we have not only returned to the premise of chapter 1 with its focus on two triangles and their related irrational numbers in the delineation of the universe; we have also returned to the beginning of creation and the formative steps that occurred prior to the creation of the four elements—earth, fire, water and air. (See [53].)

> In the first place, then, as is evident to all, fire and earth and water and air are bodies. And every sort of body possesses solidity, and every solid must necessarily be contained in planes; and every plane rectilinear figure is composed of triangles; and all triangles are originally of two kinds, both of which are made up of one right and two acute angles; one of them has at either end of the base the half of a divided right angle, having equal sides, while in the other the right angle is divided into unequal parts, having unequal sides. These, then, proceeding by a combination of probability with demonstration, we assume to be the original elements of fire and the other bodies; but the principles which are prior to these God only knows, and he of men who is the friend God.

I have no doubt tested the patience of the reader with all of this, and for that I apologize. However, all of this is important as it describes the nature of the bonds between matter in the universe. I could have saved a lot of effort by avoiding number altogether as geometry could have been used to describe all this, but number, "essence" as Timaeus calls it, is much easier and more logical for reason to comprehend.

In geometric terms, the proportions between matter are as follows: four equilateral triangles

---

[37] Wikipedia, "Platonic Solids," Platonic solid - Wikipedia. See "radii, area, and volume."

(fire) are to eight equilateral triangles (wind) as eight equilateral triangles (air) are to twenty equilateral triangles (water) as twenty equilateral triangles water are to one cube (earth). Much more concise, but it can be made more so by substituting the words with the geometric shapes themselves. Or we can do as Timaeus did by shortening it still further by using the names of the elements.

> (as fire is to air so is air to water, and as air is to water so is water to earth); and thus he bound and put together a visible and tangible heaven. And for these reasons, and out of such elements which are in number four, the body of the world was created, and it was harmonized by proportion, and therefore has the spirit of friendship; and having been reconciled to itself, was indissoluble by any other than the framer.

Regardless, is there any order or logic to be discerned in all of this? Perhaps. Consider the following.

- If we total the values assigned to the elements (6.829, 13.568, 34.64, and 24), the sum is approximately 79. If in turn we divide this by 6, the result is 13.166, which is the value of the mass of Earth in pounds ($13.166 \cdot 10^{25}$).
- If we multiply the value of water, 34.64, by 75, the result is 2,598, which is the value of the volume of Earth in cubic miles ($2.598 \cdot 10^{11}$).
- From mass and volume, the surface area of Earth can be derived: 25.98/13.166 = 1.97326, which when multiplied by (10^8), gives the Earth's surface area in square miles (the actual value is 1.9694 (10^8) square miles).[38]

But is not the foregoing a mix of different scales, six for mass and seventy-five for volume? Yes. Is it reliable? Of course. All of measurement is present. The underlying pattern in all this is in the pattern we discussed earlier; see chapter 3, "Number—The Essence of Creation." How then are we to proceed with such indefinite and ever-changing guidelines? Where is the logic in all this?

In this particular section of Timaeus, never forget where we are in creation's sequence and what step we are on. Are we not at the very beginning, before Earth and the universe were even given their spherical shapes? Did the creator not harmonize undifferentiated, formless matter before proceeding? Of course. That is why all we can logically discern of creation at this step is that it is harmonized.

---

[38] Wikipedia, "Earth," Earth – Wikipedia. accessed April 3, 2021. See measures in the side column.

Thus he bound and put together a visible and tangible heaven. And for these reasons, and out of such elements which are in number four, the body of the world was created, and it was harmonized by proportion, and therefore has the spirit of friendship; and having been reconciled to itself, it was indissoluble by the hand of any other than the framer.

But is there not also essence or number to be found in creation at this point? Otherwise, how can harmony even be discerned and analyzed? These good questions raise some of the issues with Timaeus that I did not and could not raise earlier in this narrative; his text is a jumble throughout. The earlier steps in the sequence of his narrative requires information that does not become available until later sections, and his later sections often harken back to earlier sections. His narrative seems logically arranged—for a while—and then he reverses himself and goes back to an earlier section adding more detail, yet he never seems to provide all of it until his narrative is all but complete. It is extremely challenging to the reader. And yet, if he were to relate things in a firm chronological sequence providing sufficient information and detail at each step, virtually all of it would have to be available at the very beginning, which is not possible. This is all very perplexing and begs any number of questions. There is a simple explanation though.

Timaeus did the best he was capable of in organizing and presenting his narrative, and we have done our best at following and understanding it. However, as much as we may feel the need for a more orderly, logical presentation, there is no chronological order, no logical sequence of events to be followed here because God is not in time; we are. Chronology and a sequence of events both arise from time; without it, they are meaningless and incomprehensible. So if God is not in time, he is not bound by chronology or a predetermined sequence of events. Instead, in creation, God literally proceeded from every aspect of it all at once, something we cannot conceive of. And because God is not in time, creation followed no chronology or sequence. Remember, God created time by imparting movement to his creation only *after* he had completed it. However, even this simple explanatory statement relies on chronology and sequence, does it not? But how else can we relate the act of creation so that there is logic to it without reference to a chronology and an orderly sequence of events? Is it any wonder then that Timaeus is such a jumble? Consider again section [38] and note the first sentence of the second paragraph.

When the father creator saw the creature which he had made moving and living, the created image of the eternal gods, he rejoiced, and in his joy determined to make the copy still more like the original; and as this was eternal, he sought to make the universe eternal, so far as might be. *Now the nature of the ideal being was everlasting, but to bestow this attribute in its fulness upon a creature was impossible.* Wherefore he resolved to have a moving image of eternity, and when he set in order the heaven, he made this image eternal but moving according to number, while eternity itself rests in unity; and this image we call time. For there were no days and nights and months and years before the heaven was created, but when he constructed the heaven he created them also. They are all parts of time, and the past and future are created species of time, which we unconsciously but wrongly transfer to the eternal essence; for we say that he "was," he "is," he "will be," but the truth is that "is" alone is properly attributed to him, [38] and that "was" and "will be" only to be spoken of becoming in time, for they are motions, but that which is immovably the same cannot become older or younger by time, nor ever did or has become, or hereafter will be, older or younger, nor is subject at all to any of those states which affect moving and sensible things and of which generation is the cause. These are the forms of time, which imitates eternity and revolves according to a law of number. Moreover, when we say that what has become is become and what becomes is becoming, and that what will become is about to become and that the non-existent is non-existent—all these are inaccurate modes of expression. But perhaps this whole subject will be more suitably discussed on some other occasion.

Time, then, and the heaven came into being at the same instant in order that, having been created together, if ever there was to be a dissolution of them, they might be dissolved together. It was framed after the pattern of the eternal nature, that it might resemble this as far as was possible; for the pattern exists from eternity, and the created heaven has been, and is, and will be, in all time. Such was the mind and thought of God in the creation of time. (emphasis added)

Here we will take our leave of harmony. "Perhaps this whole subject will be more suitably discussed on some other occasion."

CHAPTER 11

Soul and Radiant Energy—Measures of the Speed of Light and Gravity

Of all the issues in Timaeus, the possible connection between his use of the terms *soul* and *energy* is the most fraught with intentional vagueness as discussed in chapter 9. Even more problematic then is any effort at measuring soul, which must be possible given that soul and matter share in their binding essence or number. However, soul differs from matter as does energy; neither possesses mass. And since energy does not have mass, neither light nor gravity has mass.

> Whereas he made the soul in origin and excellence prior to and older than the body, to be the ruler and mistress, of whom the body was to be the subject. And he made her out of the following elements and on this wise: [35] Out of the indivisible and unchangeable, and also out of that which is divisible and has to do with material bodies, he compounded a third and intermediate kind of essence, partaking of the nature of the same and of the other, and this compound he placed accordingly in a mean between the indivisible, and the divisible and material.

So there are numbers with which to measure, but what numbers? Timaeus gives none specifically, but whatever they are, they too are likely to be found in the geometric progression presented and discussed in chapter 3. If soul and energy are one and the same as I have argued, the measures of energy are the measures of soul. There are several measures of energy present in this geometric progression including the speed of light, which will be our focus although not an exclusive one. But as with the other measures we have examined in light of Timaeus, these measures must express themselves not only through number but also in geometry. Let us return then to geometry.

a. The Icosahedron and the Golden Ratio

Of the four Platonic solids presented and discussed in Timaeus, only one contains a mathematical relationship found in none of the others; it is a relationship that is never specifically mentioned by Timaeus. This mathematical relationship is the golden ratio or phi as we will refer to it here. Although he never mentions phi, Timaeus undoubtedly is aware of it. As noted earlier, phi is found in only one of the four Platonic solids described in Timaeus, the icosahedron, which is the third solid he presents and the last of those formed exclusively from the triangle with dimensions based on 1, 2, and √3. On the icosahedron, phi is implied in the image of the pentagon that is readily apparent when viewing the solid from the aspect of any of its several vertices or points. It is phi that singularly distinguishes the icosahedron from the other three solids discussed in Timaeus, and it is phi that likely distinguishes soul.

I propose then that phi is one of the defining characteristics of energy and hence of soul as well. It is not the only such characteristic, but whenever and wherever it is found or implied, energy hence soul is present. No greater proof of this proposition can be found than in Earth itself, which as was discussed in chapter 1 is defined in part by the measures of √3, √2, and phi. Phi is pure essence or number; it has no materiality though it frequently expresses itself in the material world. I believe phi also expresses itself in the nonmaterial realm of soul or energy through measure.

The icosahedron as depicted in figure 14 below is composed of a series of twelve equally spaced vertices that are each made up of five equilateral triangles with the same dimensions each joined along the length of one common side with another and met at the top in a common point or vertex with the other triangles that make up each group of five in a vertex. Each such group of five equilateral triangles when viewed from the aspect of their common vertex also creates a three-dimensional image of a pentagon. However, an actual two-dimensional pentagon is not composed of equilateral triangles but of a series of 36°–54°–90° triangles.

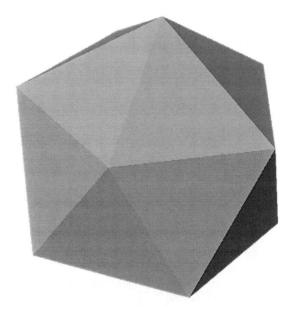

Figure 14
Icosahedron

In figure 15 (below), the pentagon image with its five-point star as depicted in the foregoing figure 14 of the icosahedron is shown inscribed in the center of the five-point star of a pentagram with a surrounding pentagon. This image is merely suggestive as the five-point star from the icosahedron with its five equilateral triangles cannot be accurately drawn on a flat surface. However, it shows that the sides of the pentagon extend outward where they intersect and form the familiar five-point star pattern. It is also noteworthy that the points of the five-point star can be linked with another to form another larger pentagon—a process that can be continued ad infinitum. This process also occurs in the opposite direction, where every pentagon can be inscribed internally with a five-point star that in turn generates another smaller pentagon. This process also continues ad infinitum.

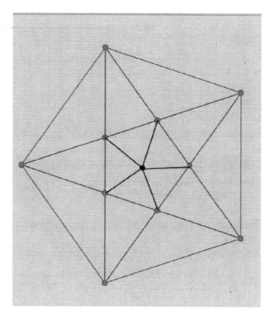

Figure 15

Pentagon with five-point star and equilateral triangles from icosahedron in center

The phi relationship of the five-point star is well documented. Every line in the pattern is intersected by another in an exact phi relationship. And as the star pattern continues internally and externally with respect to their surrounding pentagon shape, the phi relationship although smaller or larger by turn also continues ad infinitum.

Another feature of the five-point star pattern is that each arm of the star, defined as a line drawn from point to point, defines the square of phi as it is equal to phi plus one. As far as I know, this is a unique relationship in the world of mathematics. Effectively then, each arm of the star is the square of the one internal to it. Conversely, each arm of the star drawn internal to the outer one is the square root of the outer one, $\sqrt{phi^2}$ is phi. This is illustrated in figure 16 below.

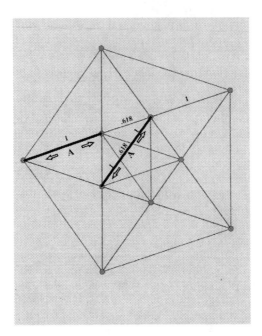

Figure 16

Pentagram with five-point star and golden ratio relations

Line A of the smaller star is exactly equal in length to the actual length of line A of the larger star; hence, the numerical measure of the length of line A of the smaller star is 2.618, or phi squared (1.618^2), which is in turn equal to the numerical measure of 1 on line A of the larger star. The numerical measure of the star's arms, defined as the line from point to the point opposite of the smaller star, is 2.618 or phi squared. The numerical measure of the star's arms of the larger star is also 2.618 or phi squared. Importantly, the numerical measure of the star's arms of the next iteration of the star that can be drawn as the pentagram is expanded outwards is always phi squared, 2.618, times the numerical measure of the arms of the previous star. (These numbers are called Lucas numbers; see table in appendix 2.)

However, never forget that phi and the various measures discussed here are numerical relationships. Other numbers can be and invariably are applied to scale the phi relationship up or down in actual practice of which there is no more apropos example of this than creation itself. And since pi, which is so critical to almost all measure, is also rooted in phi (see chapter 1), all measures that rely on pi are also scalable phi relationships.

b. The Speed of Light and the Golden Ratio

The measures of the speed of light constant, c, and the universal gravitational constant, G, are two of the most important universal constants in science.[39] Both are units in the Système International d'unités (SI) bureau of standards.

---

[39] Wikipedia, "Physical Constants," <u>Physical constant - Wikipedia.</u> accessed November 11, 2021

In international units, the speed of light in a vacuum is 9.83571056 x 108 ft s-1 or 186,282.396969 miles s-1; and the universal gravitational constant is 1.068846 · 10-9 ft3 lb-1 s-2.[40] The origins of these measures will be demonstrated; both are related to phi, the golden ratio, and both can be derived from the icosahedron and/or its five-point star pattern. Both begin with the equilateral triangle of the icosahedron and are developed through the five-point star that radiates outward from the triangle. (See figure 15.) However, it should be recalled that neither light nor gravity has mass, characteristics that they apparently share with Timaeus's concept of soul as not having a material body.

> Now when the Creator had framed the soul according to his will, he formed within her the corporeal universe, and brought the two together, and united them centre to centre. The soul, interfused everywhere from the centre to the circumference of heaven, of which also she is the external envelopment, herself turning in herself, began a divine beginning of never ceasing and rational life enduring throughout all time. [37] *The body of heaven is visible, but the soul is invisible, and partakes of reason and harmony, and being made by the best of intellectual and everlasting natures, is the best of things created.* And because she is composed of the same and of the other and of the essence, these three, and is divided and united in due proportion, and in her revolutions returns upon herself, the soul, when touching anything which has essence, whether dispersed in parts or undivided, is stirred through all her powers, to declare the sameness or difference of that thing and some other; and to what individuals are related, and by what affected, and in what way and how and when, both in the world of generation and in the world of immutable being. (emphasis added)

The speed of light begins with the speed of light from the pattern (see figure 4), which is 186,624 miles/sec. This measure differs from the actual figure by 342 miles or +0.00183593 percent. If the height of the equilateral triangle, from which light is assumed to originate, is 1.8 (more on this measure later), the half-base measure is 1.8 divided by $\sqrt{3}$ (or 1.7320508), which equals 1.03923049. The whole base measure in turn is twice this value or 2.07846098. If this measure, 2.07846098, is squared, we obtain 4.32, which if squared in turn yields 18.6624, the root number for the speed of light from the pattern 186,624. Alternatively, if we raise the square of phi, 2.618034, to the twelfth power, 2.618034^{12}, we obtain 103,682, which when multiplied by 1.8 (the height of the equilateral triangle that was assigned earlier in this section) results in

---

[40] Fundamental Physical Constants and Useful Information: Table/Constants.html (mhhe.com). accessed November 11, 2021. See "General Constants."

186,627.6, approximately equal to the measure of the speed of light from the pattern 186,624. The number 2.618034[12] represents the twelfth iteration or outward expansion of the star arms from the five-point star pattern (see figure 16).

Interestingly, if we take the precise, irrational numbers generated from the square (1.4142135) and golden rectangle (phi—1.272) from the icosahedron as was done earlier and multiply them together (1.4142135 · 1.272), the product is 1.79888. If this number is divided by √3 or 1.7320508, the result is 1.0385385678. If this number is doubled and squared as was done in the earlier procedure, the result is 4.3146257. If this number is squared again, the result is 18.6160, which when multiplied by 10,000 is 186,160. Compare this number—186,160—with the actual speed of light—186,282—a difference of 122 miles per second. (Note that these numbers, √phi, √2, and the √3, are the same as appeared in chapter 1.)

We obviously have two methods for determining the measure of the speed of light. Both are rooted in the icosahedron's structure, but only the second explicitly relies on phi for its calculation. What is the significance of this? The speed of light is constant; it does not accelerate or decelerate. It begins moving at 186,624 (precisely 186,282) miles per second from the instant it is emitted and continues at that speed outward forever.

As stated earlier, the height of the equilateral triangle, 1.8, determines the speed of light at its source, while the twelfth iteration or power of the arm of the five-point star surrounding the triangle's associated pentagon, 2.618034[12], when multiplied by 1.8 determines its outward speed at an elapsed time of 1 second. Both measures are the same. But where does 1.8 come from? If we multiply √2 · √phi or (1.4142135) (1.2720191), we get 1.7989, which is extremely close to 1.8, within .0011 or .0006 percent. This solution strongly suggests that the measure 1.8 originates from the icosahedron's internal structures with their squares and derivative golden rectangles with their phi relationship. In figure 17 below, note that each side of the smaller sides of the golden rectangles is a side of a surface equilateral triangle of the icosahedron, which as discussed in the foregoing paragraph is equal to 2.07847098.[41]

---

[41] By Fropuff, Mysid - Generated in Mathematica by w:User:Fropuff and vectorized in CorelDraw by w:User:Mysid., Public Domain, https://commons.wikimedia.org/w/index.php?curid=1335235 acessed November 11, 2021

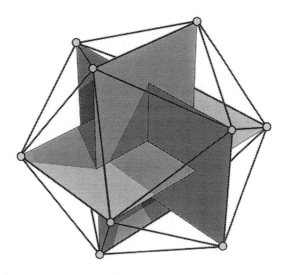

Figure 17

The squares and golden rectangles formed internally by the icosahedron

c. The Universal Constant of Gravitation and the Golden Ratio

The universal gravitational constant also begins with the equilateral triangle of the icosahedron. If the half-base of the triangle is given as 1/phi or 1/1.618034, the half-base measure is .618034, which when multiplied by $\sqrt{3}$ (1.7320508) is 1.070466, the height of the triangle. This number 1.070466 compares with the actual measure of the universal gravitational constant, 1.068846, a difference of .0016203, or +.0015156 percent. There is no pattern number (see figure 4) that is reasonably close to this number, but 1.08 comes the closest. There is no other method for calculating the universal gravitational constant as there is for calculating the speed of light.

There is a final point to be made about the universal gravitational constant. The phi measure that the universal gravitational constant is derived from is 1/phi, .0618034, the measure of the half-base of the triangle as discussed earlier. The full-base measure of this triangle is 2 · .618034, 1.236 or approximately 1.23. This is a widely encountered number in phi relationships. For example,

- $\sqrt{5} - 1 = 2/\text{phi}. = 1.236$.
- The five-point star is made up of triangles having internal angles equal to 36°–54°–90°. With a side adjacent equal to 100 and a side opposite equal to 72, the hypotenuse is equal to 123.6. (100 ÷ cos 36° = 123.6). Also, cos 36° = .809017 = phi/2. (The many phi relationships of the five-point star itself have already been discussed.)

- Phi^2 or 2.618034 raised to the fifth power, or $(2.618034)^5$, yields 122.9919.
- And finally: $\sqrt[4]{}$ ($\sqrt{2}$ · phi) or $\sqrt[4]{}$ (1.4142135 · 1.6180339) = 1.2299165897. This instance of the number is significant, because it consists of two of the three factors that defined the circumference of earth and pi. (See chapter 1.)

The main problem, though hardly the only one, with my argument is that phi may not be a unique and distinguishing characteristic of soul or energy. Matter often reflects phi, and it can frequently be observed and measured in material bodies. Therefore, the mere presence of phi in light and gravity measures is not definitive proof that soul is synonymous with energy.

As Timaeus observed, soul is diffused throughout the universe including in material bodies and likely cannot be observed in isolation. And the same likely holds true for energy. In my opinion though, the measure of the speed of light using the five-point star pattern comes very close to pure phi (soul/energy), but it still relies upon the measure of 1.8 from the internal structures of the icosahedron, which may involve materiality. However, my proposition that energy and soul are synonymous is unproven though there is one final and potentially relevant matter to be addressed: the fine-structure constant of quantum mechanics, which will be examined in the next chapter.

CHAPTER 12

The Fine-Structure Constant

The fine-structure constant is one of the principal constants of quantum mechanics, a branch of physics that deals with subatomic particles. The fine-structure constant is often called the coupling constant or measure of the electromagnetic force, which determines how electrically charged particles such as electrons and photons interact. It is also understood as a measure of the permittivity and permeability of a vacuum, which allows these particles to oscillate and move. It is thought by some to be one of the defining principles of creation.

Quantum mechanics is in one respect a fairly straightforward field of physics, but in another, it includes a number of anomalous aspects that defy the normal laws of physics and appear to border on the metaphysical. A quick read of the double-slit experiment with photons will be eye-opening for those not familiar with quantum mechanics.[42] For those who are familiar with quantum mechanics, it is still a source of wonder. It is as if these particles of energy might have sentience or aspects of intelligent life. If this is credible—and the issue is unresolved at present—might not energy be possessed of soul or be synonymous with soul? An interesting possibility, but for the moment, there is another issue that must be addressed.

Are the laws of physics in some respects different on the atomic level than they are on the cosmic level, which seems to be the case at present? Let us turn to Earth and the heavens to look for evidence of one such aspect of quantum mechanics, the fine-structure constant, to see if it is also present on a cosmic scale. If there is such evidence, it would tend to show that quantum mechanics may not have its own unique laws and constants. More broadly, it might suggest that if sentience exists in energy forms on the atomic level, it may also be present on the cosmic level. In other words, energy may be possessed of soul or could be synonymous with soul, which has been our quest for several chapters now. To begin …

a. Earth's Elliptical Orbit

---

42 Wikipedia, "Physical Constants," Physical constant - Wikipedia. accessed November 11, 2021

The orbital path of Earth traces an ellipse that is approximately 584,000,000 miles in perimeter. The semi-minor axis of this ellipse is approximately 93,000,000 miles (actual 92,956,000 miles), which is defined as the astronomical unit. Technically, the AU is defined by the average of the aphelion or farthest distance of the Sun on the semi-major axis and the perihelion or closest distance of the Sun on the semi-minor axis; however, at the equinoxes, Earth is approximately one AU from the Sun. This is equivalent to approximately 500 light-seconds (actually 499 light-seconds) using the speed of light, c, of approximately 186,282 miles/second.[43] If Earth's orbit were a circle, it would have a diameter of approximately 1,000 light-seconds and a circumference equal to $\pi \cdot 1{,}000$ light-seconds, 3,141.592653000 light-seconds. However, Earth's orbit is a circle if the focus of its orbit is the center of mass, or barycenter, of the Sun-Earth pair. Both the Sun and Earth orbit the Sun-Earth barycenter, but for our purposes, it is only Earth's orbit we are interested in, and with respect to the Sun-Earth barycenter, it is circular.[44]

When Earth reaches the point of the semi-minor axis in its orbit around the Sun, it has reached the equinox—either vernal or autumnal—on the calendar with its equal periods of daytime and nighttime, or 43,200 seconds of daytime and 43,200 seconds of nighttime. These two time factors individually or in combination define a discrete segment of Earth's orbital time period. (An illustration of this is provided at figure 18 later in this chapter.)

These factors are related in the equation: $(\pi \cdot 1{,}000$ light-seconds)/(43,200 seconds of daytime/nighttime) with the result .072722052. Dropping the zeros and using root numbers, the equation becomes: $\pi/432 = .0072722052$. This compares almost exactly with a calculation of the fine-structure constant based on phi, which is expressed in the equation $phi^2/360$ with the result .0072723166.[45] A similar result can be obtained by dividing Earth's orbital circumference measured in light-years by the year in days, 365.24, or $\pi/365.24 = .00860$, half of which is .0043, or 43 expressed as a root number. Compare 8.6 and 4.3 with the number of seconds in the day and the half-day, 86,400 and 43,200 respectively; 432 is the square root of the pattern number for the speed of light, c, 186,624 miles/second. If we use the square root of the current value for the speed of light instead, our equation becomes $\pi/\sqrt{c} = .00727887777$.

b. Sidereal Time

The movements of Earth as measured against the celestial sphere is referred to as sidereal time. In a sidereal day, there are 23 hours, 56 minutes, and 4.1 seconds vs. the 24 hours in a solar day. A sidereal year is one sidereal day longer than a solar year though both yearly measures begin and

[43] Fundamental Physical Constants and Useful Information: Table/Constants.html (mhhe.com). accessed November 11, 2021. See "General Constants."

[44] Wikipedia, "Astronomical Unit," Astronomical unit - Wikipedia, accessed May 19, 2021.

[45] Wikipedia, "Barycenter," Barycenter - Wikipedia, accessed May 28, 2021.

end at the same instant. These two time measures are related as 366.24/365.24.[46] Accordingly, whenever we are referring to the pattern traced by Earth's motions against the background stars, sidereal time must be used.

This same pattern traces out in the heavens above Earth with the north celestial pole defining Earth and the north ecliptic pole centered above the Sun with the distance between them equal to approximately 93,000,000 miles or 500 light-seconds. (The south ecliptic pole can also be used for this purpose, but this raises the question of how the ecliptic pole can run vertically through the Sun and Earth at the same time with the horizontal plane of the ecliptic[47] as the reference for both; the answer is that they cannot. Either the Sun (heliocentric) or Earth (geocentric) ecliptic pole must be used as the vertical reference on the celestial sphere when a coordinate system is used. However, the Sun's and Earth's ecliptic poles are separated by a mere 500 light-seconds, an infinitesimally small distance when measured against the immense distances of the cosmos, where such narrowly spaced, parallel lines would meet at infinity.

Due to the Sun's apparent movement about Earth, in a geocentric coordinate system, Earth is beneath the north ecliptic pole, and to an observer on Earth, the north ecliptic pole appears to orbit around the north celestial pole. The pattern traced out in the heavens against the background of stars progresses more quickly than it does measured against Earth's movements with respect to the Sun (solar time). This is true for all measures of time using the background stars of the celestial sphere as a reference, and all such time calculations are measured in sidereal time. Sidereal time differs from solar time in another important respect—it is smoother and more evenly paced than solar time because it eliminates differences in sequential time measures that result from Earth's orbital parameters.

Our earlier equation, $\pi/432$, must then be modified by the factor 366.24/365.24 or 1.0027379257, which then becomes: $(\pi/432) \cdot 1.0027379257 = .0072921159$, which compares with the currently most widely accepted value of the fine-structure constant: .0072973525693.[48] Furthermore, if we use the equation $\pi/\sqrt{c}$ and modify it by 1.0027379257 to account for sidereal time, the result is .00729880679. Moreover, since the terms for the measures of both of our equation's factors are related to seconds of time, they mutually cancel, and like the fine-structure constant, what results is a pure number unrelated to any terms of measure.

c. Kepler's Second Law and Celestial Mechanics

The equation $\pi/\sqrt{c}$ represents the orbital circumference of Earth in light-seconds to Earth's

[46] Richard Merrick, "Phi in Quantum Mechanics," *Interference, Harmonic Research and Theory*, 26 February 2012; available at Phi in Quantum Mechanics | On the Golden Ratio (interferencetheory.com). accessed November 11, 2021

[47] Wikipedia, "Ecliptic," Ecliptic - Wikipedia, accessed May 28, 2021.

[48] Wikipedia, "Sidereal Time," Sidereal time - Wikipedia accessed May 21, 2021.

orbital path over a discrete distance as measured in 43,200 seconds. I did not relate this number to an exact measure of distance in miles because this distance varies with Earth's velocity at any point of Earth's orbit according to Kepler's Second Law. This law broadly states that Earth's velocity varies with its radius from the Sun; i.e., the closer it is, the faster its velocity, and the farther away it is, the slower its velocity, so that the area of the triangle swept by its orbit between the Sun and Earth is the same between equal intervals of time along its orbit.[49]

At the semi-minor axis, the day of the equinox, the 43,200 seconds of daylight, defines a triangle the time period of which is the same when measured at any other two points that are 43,200 seconds apart in Earth's orbit. Moreover, this measure is directly related to the measure of distance at any point in Earth's orbit when adjusted for velocity. See the following figure.

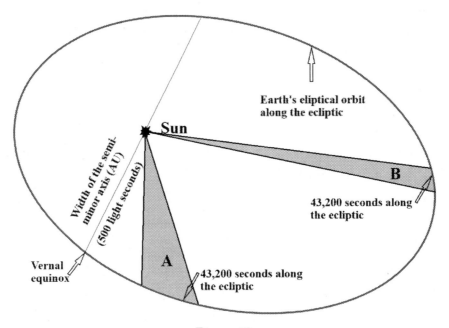

Figure 18

Illustration of Earth's elliptical orbit along the plane of the ecliptic.
(Note that the area of tringle A is equal to that of B when the times
of Earth's orbit along the base of each triangle are equal.)

This raises an interesting point. The time measure of Earth's orbit on a half-day on the day of the equinox, 43,200 seconds, is directly related to distance in that Earth travels approximately 800,000 miles during this time period. If a similar distance, 800,000 miles, is laid off along the radius with the Sun, what results is a square 43,200 seconds or 800,000 miles on a side. If the distance to the Sun is doubled, that creates a rectangle in proportion of 1 to 2—43,200 seconds or 800,000 miles to 86,400 or 1,600,000 miles. (Using the rectangular shape would accommodate

---

[49] Wikipedia, "Kepler's laws of planetary motion," <u>Kepler's laws of planetary motion - Wikipedia</u>, accessed May 24, 2021.

the aphelion and perihelion distances in Earth's orbit.) Holding the time measure along Earth's orbital path constant, the radius or distance to the Sun and Earth's velocity would all change throughout Earth's elliptical orbit. However, the area of this square or rectangle whether measured in seconds of time or in miles would stay constant in keeping with Kepler's Second Law. The area of this square or rectangle would be much easier to calculate than a triangle with a comparatively short base in relation to its far greater height if the actual distance to the Sun were used. Then substituting 431.6 for 432, the area of this square or the rectangle would become the numerical equivalent of c or 2c respectively but not the actual measure of c ($\sqrt{c} \cdot \sqrt{c} = c$ using 431.6 for $\sqrt{c}$).

So is this number that derives from the equation $(\pi/\sqrt{c}) \cdot (1.00273792570)$ or 00729880679 the same number as the fine-structure constant of quantum mechanics but one written on a cosmic scale?

The fine-structure constant of quantum mechanics deals with massless, pure-energy particles such as photons whereas astrophysics deals primarily with bodies with mass when matters of orbital mechanics etc. are considered. However, quantum mechanics does not consider orbiting electrons to be equivalent to orbiting planets though they share a number of similarities. Is this the end of our proposal? Maybe … maybe not. I don't think this question can or should be definitively addressed in this book.

d. Significance of the Fine-Structure Constant to Celestial Mechanics

Most physicists use 1/137, the inverse of .0072973525693, when making general reference to the measure of the fine-structure constant. However, disregarding decimal positions, I understand this number as 729.

The reader is no doubt wondering at the purpose of this rather tedious excursion and how it could possibly relate to Timaeus. The study of the fine-structure constant and the efforts of physicists to understand it has lasted for more than a century ever since A. Sommerfeld introduced it in 1916. In the words of physicist Richard Feynman,

> **It has been a mystery ever since it was discovered more than fifty years ago, and all good theoretical physicists put this number up on their wall and worry about it. Immediately you would like to know where this number for a coupling comes from: is it related to p or perhaps to the base of natural logarithms? Nobody knows. It's one of the greatest damn mysteries of physics: a magic number that comes to us with no understanding by man. You might say the "hand of God" wrote that number, and "we don't know how He pushed his pencil." We know what kind of a dance to do experimentally to measure this number very accurately, but we don't know what kind of dance**

to do on the computer to make this number come out, without putting it in secretly![50] **(emphasis added)**

My attempt at identifying the fine-structure constant from the motions of Earth as reflected against the background stars may or may not be convincing, but it does show that this constant may be discernible in realms beyond quantum physics. Ultimately though, even if it does withstand further scrutiny and analysis, it is not the origin of the fine-structure constant. Instead, this constant originated with the essence of creation, or number, and the pattern that derives from it. This number, as I earlier stated, is 729, and it is found in the pattern at pattern pair (0/729). The number 729 is also the cube of 9, a most important fact considering that atoms are known to resonate inside of a cube-like shell.[51] And 729 and all numbers from the pattern are pure numbers whose measures and terms are quite circumstantial depending on where they are found in the universe. Recall for example the numbers 216, 432, and 864 and their terms of measure, which were discussed in chapter 1. And recall that the numbers from the pattern are all design parameters from creation and are not the precise numbers observed and measured in the created universe.

However, as Richard Feynman suspected, it was indeed "the hand of God [that] wrote that number"—729.

How important is 729? It is one of the fundamental building blocks of the universe. That it would be found in Earth's orbit, or ecliptic, and the circle of the ecliptic as reflected in the heavens is profoundly significant but should not be surprising because this constant determines the behavior of spheres in motion and of orbiting bodies. For spherical rotating bodies, all points on the same meridian of a sphere (north-south line on a sphere running from the pole to the circumference) must turn at a proportional distance in a given time period depending on their location on the meridian. Otherwise, the sphere would tear itself apart as it rotates, and all bodies, no matter the scale—atomic or cosmic—rotate. For orbiting bodies, the space or area defined by an orbiting body's distance from its orbital focus and the time period of its orbit must be proportionally uniform throughout, i.e., they must trace out the same area just as Kepler's Second Law states to permit their orderly movement and motion in space or a vacuum; otherwise, chaos would prevail and they could well disintegrate from the forces of the orbiting motion. This is true on both the atomic and cosmic levels. And the forces involved in these motions whether electromagnetic or gravitational don't seem to matter; otherwise, there would be different

---

[50] Wikipedia, "Kepler's laws of planetary motion," Kepler's laws of planetary motion - Wikipedia, accessed May 24, 2021.

[51] Richard Merrick, "Phi in Quantum Mechanics," *Interference, Harmonic Research and Theory*, 26 February 2012; at Phi in Quantum Mechanics | On the Golden Ratio (interferencetheory.com). accessed November 11, 2021

fine-structure constants for each, would there not? But enough on this score. I cannot indulge this distraction any further without detracting from the purpose of this book.

Okay, but what is the importance of this one number to our discussion of Timaeus? Let us return to his words for guidance.

> Now when the Creator had framed the soul according to his will, he formed within her the corporeal universe, and brought the two together, and united them centre to centre. The soul, interfused everywhere from the centre to the circumference of heaven, of which also she is the external envelopment, herself turning in herself, began a divine beginning of never ceasing and rational life enduring throughout all time. [37] The body of heaven is visible, but the soul is invisible, and partakes of reason and harmony, and being made by the best of intellectual and everlasting natures, is the best of things created. *And because she is composed of the same and of the other and of the essence, these three, and is divided and united in due proportion, and in her revolutions returns upon herself, the soul, when touching anything which has essence, whether dispersed in parts or undivided, is stirred through all her powers, to declare the sameness or difference of that thing and some other; and to what individuals are related, and by what affected, and in what way and how and when, both in the world of generation and in the world of immutable being.* And when reason, which works with equal truth, whether she be in the circle of the diverse or of the same—in voiceless silence holding her onward course in the sphere of the self-moved—when reason, I say, is hovering around the sensible world and when the circle of the diverse also moving truly imparts the intimations of sense to the whole soul, then arise opinions and beliefs sure and certain. But when reason is concerned with the rational, and the circle of the same moving smoothly declares it, then intelligence and knowledge are necessarily perfected. And if anyone affirms that in which these two are found to be other than the soul, he will say the very opposite of the truth. (emphasis added)

Timaeus's words, in particular those that are emphasized, strongly suggest that soul has sentience, which is not surprising, but he clearly is discussing motions here. And motions are caused by forces, which are by nature orderly and predictable; otherwise, they would not have essence or number. But I belabor the point of my argument here and risk repeating myself to no real purpose.

I have quoted this passage of Timaeus extensively in several places in this book because in my opinion, it is one of the most insightful passages as well as one of the most difficult to fully comprehend, which may explain my repeated use of it for reference purposes. I am certain that if I could probe Timaeus's words here a little more artfully or incisively, I could learn so much more, but I cannot.

One final note. The finial or top of the north/south ecliptic pole stands directly above the plane of the ecliptic with the Sun/Earth directly at its center when measured at infinity. Here at this insignificant-looking, largely dark part of the heavens where the Sun casts its shadow in the constellation of the dragon at the north ecliptic pole and the constellation of the dolphin at the south ecliptic pole, time does not exist and never has. These two locations have stood exactly where they are since time began and will continue to do so until the end of time. They are the closest thing to the eternal that humankind can directly perceive. Here then is eternity and above it the throne of God beneath which the image of eternity turns in the unceasing motions set for it by the hand of God at the creation throughout all time. Magnificent!

CHAPTER 13

Before Time Began

Was there ever a time before God brought order and pattern to the universe, when a period of chaos existed? Logic, which operates from discrete sequential events, argues that there must have been, and indeed, Timaeus speaks of such a period at [53]. However, such a period must have occurred before time began.

Thus have I concisely given the result of my thoughts; and my verdict is that being and space and generation, these three, existed in their three ways before the heaven; and that the nurse of generation, moistened by water and inflamed by fire, and receiving the forms of earth and air, and experiencing all the affections which accompany these, presented a strange variety of appearances; and being full of powers which were neither similar nor equally balanced, was never in any part in a state of equipoise, but swaying unevenly hither and thither, was shaken by them, and by its motion again shook them; and the elements when moved were separated and carried continually, some one way, some another; as, when rain is shaken and winnowed by fans and other instruments used in the threshing of corn, [53] the close and heavy particles are borne away and settle in one direction, and the loose and light particles in another. In this manner, the four kinds or elements were then shaken by the receiving vessel, which, moving like a winnowing machine, scattered far away from one another the elements most unlike, and forced the most similar elements into dose contact. Wherefore also the various elements had different places before they were arranged so as to form the universe. At first, they were all without reason and measure. But when the world began to get into order, fire and water and earth and air had only certain faint traces of themselves, and were altogether such as everything might be expected to be in the absence of God; this, I say, was their nature at that time, and God fashioned them by form and number. Let it be consistently maintained by us in all that we say that God made them as far as possible the fairest and best, out of things which were not fair and good.

This may be true of the universe, but what of humankind? Was it created in the image of these harmonies and patterns? Yes, but ... Though humankind is composed of the same elements as the universe and these harmonies and patterns are a part of its creation, it is in a state of chaos at birth, and it is humankind's obligation to bring its soul into alignment with them.

When the creator had made all these ordinances he remained in his own accustomed nature, and his children heard and were obedient to their father's word, and receiving from him the immortal principle of a mortal creature, in imitation of their own creator they borrowed portions of fire, and earth, and water, and air from the world, [43] which were hereafter to be restored—these they took and welded them together, not with the indissoluble chains by which they were themselves bound, but with little pegs too small to be visible, making up out of all the four elements each separate body, and fastening the courses of the immortal soul in a body which was in a state of perpetual influx and efflux. Now these courses, detained as in a vast river, neither overcame nor were overcome; but were hurrying and hurried to and fro, so that the whole animal was moved and progressed, irregularly however and irrationally and anyhow, in all the six directions of motion, wandering backwards and forwards, and right and left, and up and down, and in all the six directions. For great as was the advancing and retiring flood which provided nourishment, the affections produced by external contact caused still greater tumult—when the body of any one met and came into collision with some external fire, or with the solid earth or the gliding waters, or was caught in the tempest borne on the air, and the motions produced by any of these impulses were carried through the body to the soul. All such motions have consequently received the general name of "sensations," which they still retain. And they did in fact at that time create a very great and mighty movement; uniting with the ever flowing stream in stirring up and violently shaking the courses of the soul, they completely stopped the revolution of the same by their opposing current, and hindered it from predominating and advancing; and they so disturbed the nature of the other or diverse, that the three double intervals [i.e. between 1, 2, 4, 8], and the three triple intervals [i.e. between 1, 3, 9, 27], together with the mean terms and connecting links which are expressed by the ratios of 3 : 2, and 4 : 3, and of 9 : 8—these, although they cannot be wholly undone except by him who united them, were twisted by them in all sorts of ways, and the circles were broken and disordered in every possible manner, so that when they moved they were tumbling to pieces, and moved irrationally, at one time in a reverse direction, and then again obliquely, and then upside down, as you might imagine a person who is upside down and has his head leaning upon the ground and his feet up against something in the air; and when he is in such a position, both he and the spectator fancy that the right of either is his left, and left right. If, when powerfully experiencing these and similar effects, the revolutions of the soul come in contact with some external thing, [44] either of the class of the same or of the other, they speak of the same or of the other in a manner the very opposite of the truth; and they become false and foolish, and there is no course or revolution in them which has a guiding or directing power; and if again any sensations enter in violently from without and drag after them the whole vessel of the soul, then the courses of the soul, though they seem to conquer, are really conquered.

And by reason of all these affections, the soul, when encased in a mortal body, now, as in the beginning, is at first without intelligence; but when the flood of growth and nutriment abates, and the courses of the soul, calming down, go their own way and become steadier as time goes on, then the several circles return to their natural form, and their revolutions are corrected, and they call the same and the other by their right names, and make the possessor of them to become a rational being. And if these combine in him with any true nurture or education, he attains the fulness and health of the perfect man, and escapes the worst disease of all; but if he neglects education he walks lame to the end of his life, and returns imperfect and good for nothing to the world below. This, however, is a later stage; at present we must treat more exactly the subject before us, which involves a preliminary enquiry into the generation of the body and its members, and as to how the soul was created—for what reason and by what providence of the gods; and holding fast to probability, we must pursue our way.

It is clearly humankind's obligation to calm the chaos in its soul, but why does it bear this burden? This question and others have tormented humankind since its creation and have resulted in the greatest evils imaginable. Why is the harmony of God's creation not more visible? Why do the perfect patterns of God's creation not manifest themselves more clearly and more often to us if they are necessary for us to overcome the chaos in our souls? Why didn't God perfect us in the image of these harmonies and patterns at the moment of humankind's creation? And if it is to be our burden to calm our souls and bring order to them according to these universal harmonies and patterns, what is God's purpose in this?

Furthermore, why do some believe that it is their obligation to reshape humanity in the image of their ideals of what the human race should be, and what makes humankind so susceptible to their ministrations?

Finally, why does all this doubt and confusion—chaos—cloud our vision of the eternal and lead inevitably to the greatest sin of all, the denial of God? Apparently, none of these questions has been answered satisfactorily, and it remains our obligation to bring our souls into harmony with the universe.

CHAPTER 14

Measures of the Foot and Mile

The foot of 304.8mm is believed to have originated sometime between 1266 and 1303, but there is a great deal of uncertainty surrounding its exact origin and measure.[52] It did not acquire its metric measure until 1824. The mile of 5,280 feet is reliably dated to an act of parliament during Queen Elizabeth's reign, in 1593, "An Act against converting of great Houses into several Tenements, and for the Restraint of Inmates and Inclosures, in and near the City of London and Westminster," which specified that "a Mile shall contain eight Furlongs, every furlong forty Poles, and every Pole shall contain sixteen Foot and an half" [sic].[53] The pole is understood as a rod, the modern term for this measure, and one that will be used hereafter. The rod was the principal measure for land surveys, which made it one of the most important measures as it determined land titles and taxes.[54]

a. The Measures of the Rod

As will be demonstrated, the measure of the rod has remained remarkably stable since time immemorial regardless of the terms used to define it. It is 16.5 international feet of 304.8mm (hereafter referred to as the international foot) or 15 of the old feet, meaning the Belgic or Anglo-Saxon foot of 335.28mm, which was 11/10 of the international foot.[55] Of the three known measures for the foot used in England throughout history, two are exact integers of the rod while the third one, the international foot measure, was accurate to within half an integer. Only the measure of the international foot is known for certain while the other two, the Roman foot of

---

[52] Wikipedia, "Foot (Unit)," Foot (unit) - Wikipedia, accessed April 26, 2021. See also linked material under section "England."

[53] Wikipedia, "Weights and Measures Acts," Weights and Measures Acts (UK) - Wikipedia, accessed April 26, 2021.

[54] Wikipedia, "Rod (Unit)" Rod (unit) - Wikipedia, accessed April 26, 2021.

[55] Wikipedia, "Foot (Unit)" https://en.wikipedia.org/wiki/Foot_(unit) see "England." accessed November 11, 2021

approximately 295.9mm[56] and the Belgic foot of approximately 335.28mm, are not known with certainty. However, the measure of the Belgic foot, since it is defined in terms of the international foot, is fairly certain to the extent that the Belgic foot was defined and used in Britain—an important qualifier since the Belgic foot was apparently in fairly widespread use in northern Europe as well, where its measure differed however sightly.

Comparing the three measures of the rod, then, there are,

- 15 Belgic feet of 335.28mm in a rod,
- 16.5 international feet of 304.8mm in a rod, and
- 17 Roman feet of 295.84mm in a rod (generally accepted measure is 295.9mm).

A couple of observations can be made from these comparisons. One, regardless of who ruled Britain whether Belgians, Romans, or Anglo-Saxons, the measures they brought with them to Britain were readily defined in terms of the rod thus permitting continuity for land measures and taxes. And two, these measures are all too perfect and remarkably symmetrical, which suggests that the rod may have been their common source as implausible as that may seem.

However, there is another measure to be analyzed—the Neolithic or long foot, 321.8688mm, which has been found at Stonehenge as well as a number of other sites and on artifacts dating from the Neolithic age in Britain. Of particular note in this regard, the lintels above the standing stones at Stonehenge were determined to measure 10 long feet or 10.56 international feet of 304.8mm.[57] Many of the ruins measured have demonstrated that the long foot is often used in increments of thirty, but this measure has not been attested to beyond Britain.

b. The Rod and Stonehenge

The long foot may indeed be a measure used in Neolithic times in Britain, but it is a measure that can readily be related to the modern rod of 16.5 international feet. Using the measure of the length of a Stonehenge lintel, 10 long feet or 3218.688mm, and dividing it by the international foot of 304.8mm, the length of the lintel then is equal to 10.56 international feet. If 10.56 international feet are divided by 16.5 international feet in a rod, the result is 0.64 rods or 64 percent of a rod. Thus each lintel at Stonehenge in the great inner circle of standing sarsens is 0.64 rods, and since there are thirty lintels in the circle actual or implied, the circumference of the circle

---

[56] Wikipedia, "Ancient Roman Units of Measure," https://en.wikipedia.org/wiki/Ancient_Roman_units_of_measurement#:~:text=Ancient%20Roman%20units%20of%20length%20%20%20,%200.728%20ft%20%20 11%20more%20rows%20 accessed April 26, 2021

[57] Wikipedia, "Foot (Unit)" See section "England." Foot (unit) - Wikipedia, Also see Anne Teather, "Getting the Measure of Stonehenge" *British Archaeology* magazine (March/April 2019): 48–51.

is 19.2 rods. Of particular note here is the measure of 0.64 rods with the root number 64, which is directly related to the diameter of the Sun as will be discussed in the following paragraphs.

c. Significance of the Number 64

A common rule of thumb is that the mean apparent diameters of the Moon and Sun are related as 31.5 arc-minutes (actual is 31.6) to 32 arc-minutes (actual is 32) or 63:64 or .984375 (actual is .9875).[58] However, 63:64 is accurate enough for most purposes. But the mean apparent diameter of the Sun is 32 arc-minutes, not 64, a major but not insurmountable discrepancy. The design and purpose of the lintels likely dictated their dimensions, which necessitated that their length be doubled—a convincing but hardly definitive answer.

There is another clue to the intentional use of the 0.64 dimension from a very ancient culture thousands of miles from Britain—ancient Egypt.

One of ancient Egypt's most iconic symbols is the eye of Horus depicted below with its fractional components.

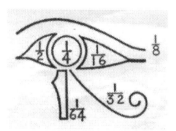

Figure 19

Eye of Horus with fractions

The Eye of Horus, or *wedjat* eye, is most often identified as the left eye or damaged eye of Horus, and it is frequently associated with the Moon, while the right eye or hale eye is usually identified with Re and the Sun.[59] The Eye of Horus is often depicted in fractional parts as shown above, and its fractions add up to 63/64. Sir Alan Gardiner calls this number the "corn measure" and comments on the missing 1/64th part as being "supplied magically by Thoth." Gardiner identifies these fractions with the *ḥeḳat*-measure of volumes.[60] Gardiner's association in this respect is very relevant because as many metrologists understand, almost all volume measures have their origin in linear measures.

---

[58] U.S. National Aeronautics and Space Administration (NASA) "Sun Fact Sheet," Sun Fact Sheet (nasa.gov). Mean apparent diameter is 1,919.5 arc-seconds or 32 arc-minutes. "Moon Fact Sheet" Moon Fact Sheet (nasa.gov). accessed November 11, 2021. Mean apparent diameter is 1,896 arc-seconds or 31.6 arc- minutes.

[59] Wikipedia, "Eye of Horus," https://en.wikipedia.org/wiki/Eye_of_Horus accessed April 30, 2021.

[60] Sir Alan Gardiner, *Egyptian Grammar; Being an Introduction to the Study of Hieroglyphs*; third edition, revised 2005 (Griffith Institute, Oxford: University Press, Cambridge) § 266, 197–98.

Furthermore, it is very noteworthy for our purposes that the 63/64 relationship embodied in the Eye of Horus measure is identical to the relationship of the mean apparent diameters of the Sun and Moon as described earlier, also 63/64. It is also quite noteworthy that Stonehenge has long been associated with the Sun and in particular the marking of the summer solstice, so the presence of the number 64 in the measure of some of its structures is not mere coincidence; instead, it was by specific design. But there is much more.

The embodiment of the 63/64 measure in the Eye of Horus leads to one of the most fundamental of all linear measure relationships: 63/64 of the international foot of 304.8mm = 300.0375mm—a very precise measure of the common Egyptian foot that is widely accepted as 300mm. This measure in turn leads to the common Egyptian royal cubit of 525.065625mm.[61] (There are four hands in an Egyptian foot and seven hands in a royal cubit, thus 300.0375mm ÷ 4 = .75009375mm and .75009375mm · 7 = 525.065625mm.) The international foot of 304.8mm had to have been known to the ancient Egyptians, but they do not appear to have used it for their measurements though it is attested in one spectacular measure. Instead, the derived measures of the Egyptian foot and cubit were used as the basis for all their measures. The Egyptian measures are also very useful for geodesic measurements, but this is a vast subject in its own right and one that is far beyond the limited scope of this book.

A final question: Which of these measures came first, the Egyptian foot or the international foot? Likely both measures came into existence at the same time, and considering the demonstrable antiquity of both, they both were given to humanity at the beginning of time.

There is another observation that can be made of the Stonehenge lintel measure of 10.56 rods. If it is successively divided by 2, the first six numbers generated are 5.28, 2.64, 1.32, .66, .33, and .165. If the first three numbers in this series are multiplied by 1,000 or 10^3, the resulting numbers are 5,280, 2,640, and 1,320. In terms of the international foot, these are the exact measures of the mile, the half-mile, and the quarter-mile. If the next three numbers in this series—.66, .33, and .165—are multiplied by 100 or 10^2, the resulting numbers are 66, 33, and 16.5. In terms of the international foot, these are the exact measures of the furlong, half-furlong, and rod. That the Stonehenge monument incorporates these numbers appears to be a matter of specific design, not coincidence. Could this measure of .64 of a rod or 10.56 international feet have been used in actual practice? A difficult question for which I can offer no answer without engaging in far more analysis that would go well beyond the purposes of this book. However, it may be noteworthy in this regard that there are exactly 500 .64 rods in a mile of 5,280 international feet, which might prove useful as a unit of measure in the field.

Among its other possible purposes then, Stonehenge acts as the memorial to and the enduring archetype of the national standards of the linear measures of the British people; it is also a relic

---

[61] All measures are reduced to metric measures for ease of reference.

and memorial for all humanity. And considering the earlier discussion of the Roman and Belgic measures of the foot and their relationship to the rod, these Stonehenge measures are likely the archetypes for these measures as well. As to how the Roman and Belgic measures found their way to the sites where they are best attested, i.e., Rome, Belgium, and Germany, that is a matter of speculation as there are no relevant records to examine.

One final observation of the measure of the lintel stone. If the horizontal measure of the stone is .64 of the length of a rod (16.5 international feet) or 10.56 feet, a hypothetical, vertical, complementary measure would be .36 of the length of a rod, 5.94 feet (10.56 + 5.94 = 16.5, or 64 percent + 36 percent = 100 percent). The hypotenuse of the triangle inferred from these two measures would be 1.00, or 16.5 feet. These measures are in the ratio of the Pythagorean triangle, 3:4:5, where the measure of the vertical leg is .36, or .4 · 9 (or 3^2), the measure of the horizontal leg is .64 or .4 · 16 (or 4^2), and the measure of the hypotenuse is 1.00 or .4 · 25 (or 5^2). This Pythagorean triangle relationship would prove useful as a mnemonic device for recalling the dimensions of the stone lintel and their relationship to the measure of the rod.

This chapter's rather tedious examination of measures and numbers was necessary as it demonstrates that many of the linear measures employed by humanity were in use at extremely early ages in disparate geographical locations and that many of them appear to be very precisely coordinated with one another. This was all by specific design and could not be the result of a gradual, evolutionary development. Someone who knew Earth and its measurements in great detail gave these measurements to humanity.

d. Summary

Thus we have completed our path that has led directly from the square roots of 2 and 3 and the golden ratio to the measures of Earth's radius, diameter, and circumference used in the creation of Earth and then to humanity's knowledge of and use of these same measures. These simple, mundane numerical measures, which are so much a part of our daily lives that we invariably just take them for granted—are the very essence of Earth's creation, and they arose directly from the combination of matter and soul by the hand of God in the act of creation precisely as Timaeus claims.

CHAPTER 15

Summary and Discussion

If you have arrived at this point, you have no doubt endured a very arduous climb, having negotiated a constant and unrelenting series of numbers and geometrical figures. This would be hard when the subject matter is narrow and concise, but when the subject matter is a jumble of different scientific fields and disciplines, it is many times more so. Unfortunately, there is no other way, and as I described in some detail in chapter 10, the subject matter, which involves the creation of the universe, is extraordinarily complex and difficult to present in a logical, orderly fashion as it is almost incomprehensible to us as mere humans.

While I have tried my best, I am not sure that I have been equal to the burden of bringing about an understanding of Timaeus's account. I must recognize and thank Timaeus for his incomparable narrative; it is magnificent in every detail and masterfully concise and to the point in every respect. However, he is cryptic and vague in a number of areas—likely intentionally so—but in every instance, the details he provided were of a critical nature allowing for his message to be discerned. Timaeus everywhere in his narrative appears confident, completely in control of his subject matter, able to digress with ease where and when appropriate, and then make a timely return to his main theme. He leaves no loose ends and appears to have covered every aspect of his topic in sufficient detail so that his meaning is never ultimately in doubt.

But how was he able to master so many different scientific disciplines and see and comprehend their underlying patterns and harmony and their part in the grand design of the universe? This is in itself almost incomprehensible and raises a valid question: Is Timaeus in fact the author of this narrative or merely its scribe? If the former and it was Timaeus, he is one of the greatest figures in history and certainly one of its smartest. But how did he come to his knowledge? Where and how was he taught? It is virtually impossible for him to have been a citizen of classical Greece. (Plato is believed to have lived from 428–348 BC.) If the latter, then who was the author? This is a staggering question as this individual had to have been someone intimately familiar with the details of creation and its overarching design principles and one thoroughly versed in measures, someone who could also see and understand the underlying grand design of the universe. If it was not one of God's created lesser gods as Timaeus calls them, it had to be someone—a mere human?—intimately familiar with all aspects of creation. In my opinion, it had to have been one of the lesser gods intimately involved with creation, but who? However, unless some other evidence emerges, the author has been and should continue to be identified as Timaeus.

To know or tell the origin of the other divinities is beyond us, and we must accept the traditions of the men of old time who affirm themselves to be the offspring of the gods—that is what they say—and they must surely have known their own ancestors. How can we doubt the word of the children of the gods? Although they give no probable or certain proofs, still, as they declare that they are speaking of what took place in their own family, we must conform to custom and believe them. In this manner, then, according to them, the genealogy of these gods is to be received and set forth.

Oceanus and Tethys were the children of Earth and Heaven, and from these sprang Phorcys and Cronos and Rhea, and all that generation; [41] and from Cronos and Rhea sprang Zeus and Here, and all those who are said to be their brethren, and others who were the children of these.

Now, when all of them, both those who visibly appear in their revolutions as well as those other gods who are of a more retiring nature, had come into being, the creator of the universe addressed them in these words: "Gods, children of gods, who are my works, and of whom I am the artificer and father, my creations are indissoluble, if so I will. All that is bound may be undone, but only an evil being would wish to undo that which is harmonious and happy. Wherefore, since ye are but creatures, ye are not altogether immortal and indissoluble, but ye shall certainly not be dissolved, nor be liable to the fate of death, having in my will a greater and mightier bond than those with which ye were bound at the time of your birth. And now listen to my instructions:—Three tribes of mortal beings remain to be created—without them the universe will be incomplete, for it will not contain every kind of animal which it ought to contain, if it is to be perfect. On the other hand, if they were created by me and received life at my hands, they would be on an equality with the gods. In order then that they may be mortal, and that this universe may be truly universal, do ye, according to your natures, betake yourselves to the formation of animals, imitating the power which was shown by me in creating you. The part of them worthy of the name immortal, which is called divine and is the guiding principle of those who are willing to follow justice and you—of that divine part I will myself sow the seed, and having made a beginning, I will hand the work over to you. And do ye then interweave the mortal with the immortal, and make and beget living creatures, and give them food, and make them to grow, and receive them again in death.

Two timely questions: Could the author be God? Was this narrative written and provided to humankind so it might make itself more familiar with those harmonies and patterns of the universe, which is incumbent upon it to learn to help it rid its soul of chaos? As to the first question, it is highly unlikely that God was the author of this text. If God handed off much of creation to the lesser gods as Timaeus states, he almost certainly handed off the authorship of this text as well. As to the second question—providing a means for humankind to rid its soul of chaos—this was likely the principal intended purpose of the text.

There are any number of chronological problems with Timaeus's text none of which are resolvable in terms of the widely accepted chronology of the human race and most especially the history of various civilizations. How could any ancient civilization accumulate such a broad understanding of life and the cosmos given the documented scientific achievements of ancient civilizations? They could not and did not. And how could any one member of any ancient civilization come to such knowledge? Such a human being likely never existed. Also, to say that Timaeus is at significance variance with many scientific theories regarding the origin of Earth, the solar system, and the cosmos is an extreme understatement. However, is there really conflict here, or is it simply a matter of our acknowledging God's presence in his creation? Also, if Timaeus's text was an inherited manuscript from an impossibly older time, there is no chronological conflict.

Timaeus has presented his case and proved it; it can be challenged, but I believe it will withstand any challenge. Much of his narrative, the part that I have covered anyhow, relies on number and geometry, which are hard facts to overcome. And if my interpretations are erroneous, it is up to critics to say so and be specific as to how they are erroneous. "It simply can't be" is not an argument. And if the critics' argument is that my figures are not precise, I will remind them that Timaeus's figures and my interpretations of them are indicative of an underlying pattern and its harmonies and that these are the source for creation, not the as-built measures, which I have conceded at the outset are accurate in every respect to the extent modern science can render them so.

I have not and will not challenge any of them. In fact, I do not believe there is any conflict between the pattern and modern scientific measures. It is my hope that many scientists may see something in all this that they may have always suspected existed but never fully grasped because the pressures of scientific inquiry demanded that their research and scholarship be narrow and focused. This is not a criticism; theirs is an approach that has allowed for the many scientific breakthroughs that have defined modern civilization. The pattern and the harmonies they encompass are the underlying unity of all creation. And, unlike the as-built dimensions and measures of the world around us, the pattern is perfect—as Timaeus claims.

I have delved into only those parts of Timaeus in the first half of his narrative that are related to the cosmic aspects of creation because a great deal of this text rests in number and geometry, which have been particularly viewed as enigmatic and cryptic throughout the known history of the narrative. I hope my services as a guide have been beneficial to readers in these matters though even my explanations are difficult to comprehend. However, I recognize that this was shortsighted on my part as the smaller aspects of creation, which are largely the focus of the second half of his narrative, were formed by the same forces that were at play on the cosmic level. But as the telling of the tale from its cosmic perspective seemed such a specialized and difficult undertaking, I arbitrarily split the two aspects of the tale and focused exclusively on the first half, the more difficult of the two. The second part of the tale is every bit as relevant as the first, and as I said, they are both parts of the same tale, which is the act of creation and the nature of the created universe. The second part of the narrative though is largely devoid of number, and its text is much easier to negotiate and comprehend. A guide is quite unnecessary here as Timaeus speaks quite clearly and eloquently for himself. I could add nothing to his words.

Finally, I conclude with the words of Johannes Kepler in his seminal work, *Harmonius Mundi*,

Accordingly let this do for our *envoi* concerning the work of God the Creator. It now remains that at last, with my eyes and hands removed from the tablet of demonstrations and lifted up towards the heavens, I should pray, devout and supplicating, to the Father of lights: O Thou Who dost by the light of nature promote in us the desire for the light of grace, that by its means Thou mayest transport us into the light of glory, I give thanks to Thee, O Lord Creator, Who hast delighted me with Thy makings and in the works of Thy hands have I exalted. Behold! now, I have completed the work of my profession, having employed as much power of mind as Thou didst give to me; to the men who are going to read those demonstrations I have made manifest the glory of Thy works, as much of its infinity as the narrows of my intellect could apprehend. My mind has been given over to philosophizing most correctly: if there is anything unworthy of Thy designs brought forth by me—a worm born and nourished in a wallowing place of sins—breathe into me also that which Thou dost wish men to know, that I may make the correction: If I have been allured into rashness by the wonderful beauty of Thy works, or if I have loved my own glory among men, while I am advancing in the work destined for Thy glory, be gentle and merciful and pardon me; and finally deign graciously to effect that these demonstrations give way to Thy glory and the salvation of souls and nowhere be an obstacle to that.

—Johannes Kepler, *Harmonious Mundi*, 1619

Appendix 1

TIMAEUS

Provided by The Internet Classics Archive.
Available online at
http://classics.mit.edu//Plato/timaeus.html

Timaeus
By Plato

Translated by Benjamin Jowett

Persons of the Dialogue
SOCRATES
CRITIAS
TIMAEUS
HERMOCRATES

----

[17] Socrates. One, two, three; but where, my dear Timaeus, is the fourth of those who were yesterday my guests and are to be my entertainers to-day?

Timaeus. He has been taken ill, Socrates; for he would not willingly have been absent from this gathering.

Soc. Then, if he is not coming, you and the two others must supply his place.

Tim. Certainly, and we will do all that we can; having been handsomely entertained by you yesterday, those of us who remain should be only too glad to return your hospitality.

Soc. Do you remember what were the points of which I required you to speak?

Tim. We remember some of them, and you will be here to remind us of anything which we have forgotten: or rather, if we are not troubling you, will you briefly recapitulate the whole, and then the particulars will be more firmly fixed in our memories?

Soc. To be sure I will: the chief theme of my yesterday's discourse was the State- how constituted and of what citizens composed it would seem likely to be most perfect.

Tim. Yes, Socrates; and what you said of it was very much to our mind.

Soc. Did we not begin by separating the husbandmen and the artisans from the class of defenders of the State?

Tim. Yes.

Soc. And when we had given to each one that single employment and particular art which was suited to his nature, we spoke of those who were intended to be our warriors, and said that they were to be guardians of the city against attacks from within as well as from without, *[18]* and to have no other employment; they were to be merciful in judging their subjects, of whom they were by nature friends, but fierce to their enemies, when they came across them in battle.

Tim. Exactly.

Soc. We said, if I am not mistaken, that the guardians should be gifted with a temperament in a high degree both passionate and philosophical; and that then they would be as they ought to be, gentle to their friends and fierce with their enemies.

Tim. Certainly.

Soc. And what did we say of their education? Were they not to be trained in gymnastic, and music, and all other sorts of knowledge which were proper for them?

Tim. Very true.

Soc. And being thus trained they were not to consider gold or silver or anything else to be their own private property; they were to be like hired troops, receiving pay for keeping guard from those who were protected by them-the pay was to be no more than would suffice for men of simple life; and they were to spend in common, and to live together in the continual practice of virtue, which was to be their sole pursuit.

Tim. That was also said.

Soc. Neither did we forget the women; of whom we declared, that their natures should be assimilated and brought into harmony with those of the men, and that common pursuits should be assigned to them both in time of war and in their ordinary life.

Tim. That, again, was as you say.

Soc. And what about the procreation of children? Or rather not the proposal too singular to be forgotten? for all wives and children were to be in common, to the intent that no one should ever know his own child, but they were to imagine that they were all one family; those who were within a suitable limit of age were to be brothers and sisters, those who were of an elder generation parents and grandparents, and those of a younger children and grandchildren.

Tim. Yes, and the proposal is easy to remember, as you say.

Soc. And do you also remember how, with a view of securing as far as we could the best breed, we said that the chief magistrates, male and female, should contrive secretly, by the use of certain lots, so to arrange the nuptial meeting, that the bad of either sex and the good of either sex might pair with their like; and there was to be no quarrelling on this account, for they would imagine that the union was a mere accident, and was to be attributed to the lot?

Tim. I remember.

Soc. And you remember how we said that the children of the good parents were to be educated, *[19]* and the children of the bad secretly dispersed among the inferior citizens; and while they were all growing up the rulers were to be on the look-out,

95

and to bring up from below in their turn those who were worthy, and those among themselves who were unworthy were to take the places of those who came up?

Tim. True.

Soc. Then have I now given you all the heads of our yesterday's discussion? Or is there anything more, my dear Timaeus, which has been omitted?

Tim. Nothing, Socrates; it was just as you have said.

Soc. I should like, before proceeding further, to tell you how I feel about the State which we have described. I might compare myself to a person who, on beholding beautiful animals either created by the painter's art, or, better still, alive but at rest, is seized with a desire of seeing them in motion or engaged in some struggle or conflict to which their forms appear suited; this is my feeling about the State which we have been describing. There are conflicts which all cities undergo, and I should like to hear some one tell of our own city carrying on a struggle against her neighbours, and how she went out to war in a becoming manner, and when at war showed by the greatness of her actions and the magnanimity of her words in dealing with other cities a result worthy of her training and education. Now I, Critias and Hermocrates, am conscious that I myself should never be able to celebrate the city and her citizens in a befitting manner, and I am not surprised at my own incapacity; to me the wonder is rather that the poets present as well as past are no better-not that I mean to depreciate them; but every one can see that they are a tribe of imitators, and will imitate best and most easily the life in which they have been brought up; while that which is beyond the range of a man's education he finds hard to carry out in action, and still harder adequately to represent in language. I am aware that the Sophists have plenty of brave words and fair conceits, but I am afraid that being only wanderers from one city to another, and having never had habitations of their own, they may fail in their conception of philosophers and statesmen, and may not know what they do and say in time of war, when they are fighting or holding parley with their enemies. And thus people of your class are the only ones remaining who are fitted by nature and education to take part at once both in politics and philosophy. Here is Timaeus, *[20]* of Locris in Italy, a city which has admirable laws, and who is himself in wealth and rank the equal of any of his fellow-citizens; he has held the most important and honourable offices in his own state, and, as I believe, has scaled the heights of all philosophy; and here is Critias, whom every Athenian knows to be no novice in the matters of which we are speaking; and as to, Hermocrates, I am assured by many witnesses that his genius and education qualify him to take part in any speculation of the kind. And therefore yesterday when I saw that you wanted me to describe the formation of the State, I readily assented, being very well aware, that, if you only would, none were better qualified to carry the discussion further, and that when you had engaged our city in a suitable war, you of all men living could best exhibit her playing a fitting part. When I had completed my task, I in return imposed this other task upon you. You conferred together and agreed to entertain me to-day, as I had entertained you, with a feast of discourse. Here am I in festive array, and no man can be more ready for the promised banquet.

Her. And we too, Socrates, as Timaeus says, will not be wanting in enthusiasm; and there is no excuse for not complying with your request. As soon as we arrived yesterday at the guest-chamber of Critias, with whom we are staying, or rather on our way thither, we talked the matter over, and he told us an ancient tradition, which I wish, Critias, that you would repeat to Socrates, so that he may help us to judge whether it will satisfy his requirements or not.

Crit. I will, if Timaeus, who is our other partner, approves.

Tim. I quite approve.

Crit. Then listen, Socrates, to a tale which, though strange, is certainly true, having been attested by Solon, who was the wisest of the seven sages. He was a relative and a dear friend of my great-grandfather, Dropides, as he himself says in many passages of his poems; and he told the story to Critias, my grandfather, who remembered and repeated it to us. There were of old, he said, great and marvellous actions of the Athenian city, *[21]* which have passed into oblivion through lapse of time and the destruction of mankind, and one in particular, greater than all the rest. This we will now rehearse. It will be a fitting monument of our gratitude to you, and a hymn of praise true and worthy of the goddess, on this her day of festival.

Soc. Very good. And what is this ancient famous action of the Athenians, which Critias declared, on the authority of Solon, to be not a mere legend, but an actual fact?

Crit. I will tell an old-world story which I heard from an aged man; for Critias, at the time of telling it, was as he said, nearly ninety years of age, and I was about ten. Now the day was that day of the Apaturia which is called the Registration of Youth, at which, according to custom, our parents gave prizes for recitations, and the poems of several poets were recited by us boys, and many of us sang the poems of Solon, which at that time had not gone out of fashion. One of our tribe, either because he thought so or to please Critias, said that in his judgment Solon was not only the wisest of men, but also the noblest of poets. The old man, as I very well remember, brightened up at hearing this and said, smiling: Yes, Amynander, if Solon had only, like other poets, made poetry the business of his life, and had completed the tale which he brought with him from Egypt, and had not been compelled, by reason of the factions and troubles which he found stirring in his own country when he came home, to attend to other matters, in my opinion he would have been as famous as Homer or Hesiod, or any poet.

And what was the tale about, Critias? said Amynander. About the greatest action which the Athenians ever did, and which ought to have been the most famous, but, through the lapse of time and the destruction of the actors, it has not come down to us.

Tell us, said the other, the whole story, and how and from whom Solon heard this veritable tradition.

He replied:-In the Egyptian Delta, at the head of which the river Nile divides, there is a certain district which is called the district of Sais, and the great city of the district is also called Sais, and is the city from which King Amasis came. The citizens have a deity for their foundress; she is called in the Egyptian tongue Neith, and is asserted by them to be the same whom the Hellenes call Athene; they are great lovers of the Athenians, and say that they are in some way related to them. To this city came Solon, and was received there with great honour; [22] he asked the priests who were most skilful in such matters, about antiquity, and made the discovery that neither he nor any other Hellene knew anything worth mentioning about the times of old. On one occasion, wishing to draw them on to speak of antiquity, he began to tell about the most ancient things in our part of the world-about Phoroneus, who is called "the first man," and about Niobe; and after the Deluge, of the survival of Deucalion and Pyrrha; and he traced the genealogy of their descendants, and reckoning up the dates, tried to compute how many years ago the events of which he was speaking happened. Thereupon one of the priests, who was of a very great age, said: O Solon, Solon, you Hellenes are never anything but children, and there is not an old man among you. Solon in return asked him what he meant. I mean to say, he replied, that in mind you are all young; there is no old opinion handed down among you by ancient tradition, nor any science which is hoary with age. And I will tell you why. There have been, and will be again, many destructions of mankind arising out of many causes; the greatest have been brought about by the agencies of fire and water, and other lesser ones by innumerable other causes. There is a story, which even you have preserved, that once upon a time Paethon, the son of Helios, having yoked the steeds in his father's chariot, because he was not able to drive them in the path of his father, burnt up all that was upon the earth, and was himself destroyed by a thunderbolt. Now this has the form of a myth, but really signifies a declination of the bodies moving in the heavens around the earth, and a great conflagration of things upon the earth, which recurs after long intervals; at such times those who live upon the mountains and in dry and lofty places are more liable to destruction than those who dwell by rivers or on the seashore. And from this calamity the Nile, who is our never-failing saviour, delivers and preserves us. When, on the other hand, the gods purge the earth with a deluge of water, the survivors in your country are herdsmen and shepherds who dwell on the mountains, but those who, like you, live in cities are carried by the rivers into the sea. Whereas in this land, neither then nor at any other time, does the water come down from above on the fields, having always a tendency to come up from below; for which reason the traditions preserved here are the most ancient.

The fact is, that wherever the extremity of winter frost or of summer does not prevent, mankind exist, sometimes in greater, [23] sometimes in lesser numbers. And whatever happened either in your country or in ours, or in any other region of which we are informed-if there were any actions noble or great or in any other way remarkable, they have all been written down by us of old, and are preserved in our temples. Whereas just when you and other nations are beginning to be provided with letters and the other requisites of civilized life, after the usual interval, the stream from heaven, like a pestilence, comes pouring down, and leaves only those of you who are destitute of letters and education; and so you have to begin all over again like children, and know nothing of what happened in ancient times, either among us or among yourselves. As for those genealogies of yours which you just now recounted to us, Solon, they are no better than the tales of children. In the first place you remember a single deluge only, but there were many previous ones; in the next place, you do not know that there formerly dwelt in your land the fairest and noblest race of men which ever lived, and that you and your whole city are descended from a small seed or remnant of them which survived. And this was unknown to you, because, for many generations, the survivors of that destruction died, leaving no written word. For there was a time, Solon, before the great deluge of all, when the city which now is Athens was first in war and in every way the best governed of all cities, is said to have performed the noblest deeds and to have had the fairest constitution of any of which tradition tells, under the face of heaven.

Solon marvelled at his words, and earnestly requested the priests to inform him exactly and in order about these former citizens. You are welcome to hear about them, Solon, said the priest, both for your own sake and for that of your city, and above all, for the sake of the goddess who is the common patron and parent and educator of both our cities. She founded your city a thousand years before ours, receiving from the Earth and Hephaestus the seed of your race, and afterwards she founded ours, of which the constitution is recorded in our sacred registers to be eight thousand years old. As touching your citizens of nine thousand years ago, *[24]* I will briefly inform you of their laws and of their most famous action; the exact particulars of the whole we will hereafter go through at our leisure in the sacred registers themselves. If you compare these very laws with ours you will find that many of ours are the counterpart of yours as they were in the olden time. In the first place, there is the caste of priests, which is separated from all the others; next, there are the artificers, who ply their several crafts by themselves and do not intermix; and also there is the class of shepherds and of hunters, as well as that of husbandmen; and you will observe, too, that the warriors in Egypt are distinct from all the other classes, and are commanded by the law to devote themselves solely to military pursuits; moreover, the weapons which they carry are shields and spears, a style of equipment which the goddess taught of Asiatics first to us, as in your part of the world first to you. Then as to wisdom, do you observe how our law from the very first made a study of the whole order of things, extending even to prophecy and medicine which gives health, out of these divine elements deriving what was needful for human life, and adding every sort of knowledge which was akin to them. All this order and arrangement the goddess first imparted to you when establishing your city; and she chose the spot of earth in which you were born, because she saw that the happy temperament of the seasons in that land would produce the wisest of men. Wherefore the goddess, who was a lover both of war and of wisdom, selected and first of all settled that spot which was the most likely to produce men likest herself. And there you dwelt, having such laws as these and still better ones, and excelled all mankind in all virtue, as became the children and disciples of the gods.

Many great and wonderful deeds are recorded of your state in our histories. But one of them exceeds all the rest in greatness and valour. For these histories tell of a mighty power which unprovoked made an expedition against the whole of Europe and Asia, and to which your city put an end. This power came forth out of the Atlantic Ocean, for in those days the Atlantic was navigable; and there was an island situated in front of the straits which are by you called the Pillars of Heracles; the island was larger than Libya and Asia put together, *[25]* and was the way to other islands, and from these you might pass to the whole of the opposite continent which surrounded the true ocean; for this sea which is within the Straits of Heracles is only a harbour, having a narrow entrance, but that other is a real sea, and the surrounding land may be most truly called a boundless continent. Now in this island of Atlantis there was a great and wonderful empire which had rule over the whole island and several others, and over parts of the continent, and, furthermore, the men of Atlantis had subjected the parts of Libya within the columns of Heracles as far as Egypt, and of Europe as far as Tyrrhenia. This vast power, gathered into one, endeavoured to subdue at a blow our country and yours and the whole of the region within the straits; and then, Solon, your country shone forth, in the excellence of her virtue and strength, among all mankind. She was pre-eminent in courage and military skill, and was the leader of the Hellenes. And when the rest fell off from her, being compelled to stand alone, after having undergone the very extremity of danger, she defeated and triumphed over the invaders, and preserved from slavery those who were not yet subjugated, and generously liberated all the rest of us who dwell within the pillars. But afterwards there occurred violent earthquakes and floods; and in a single day and night of misfortune all your warlike men in a body sank into the earth, and the island of Atlantis in like manner disappeared in the depths of the sea. For which reason the sea in those parts is impassable and impenetrable, because there is a shoal of mud in the way; and this was caused by the subsidence of the island.

I have told you briefly, Socrates, what the aged Critias heard from Solon and related to us. And when you were speaking yesterday about your city and citizens, the tale which I have just been repeating to you came into my mind, and I remarked with astonishment how, by some mysterious coincidence, you agreed in almost every particular with the narrative of Solon; but I did not like to speak at the moment. *[26]* For a long time had elapsed, and I had forgotten too much; I thought that I must first of all run over the narrative in my own mind, and then I would speak. And so I readily assented to your request yesterday, considering that in all such cases the chief difficulty is to find a tale suitable to our purpose, and that with such a tale we should be fairly well provided.

And therefore, as Hermocrates has told you, on my way home yesterday I at once communicated the tale to my companions as I remembered it; and after I left them, during the night by thinking I recovered nearly the whole it. Truly, as is often said, the lessons of our childhood make wonderful impression on our memories; for I am not sure that I could remember all the discourse of yesterday, but I should be much surprised if I forgot any of these things which I have heard very long ago. I listened at the time with childlike interest to the old man's narrative; he was very ready to teach me, and I asked him again and again to repeat his words, so that like an indelible picture they were branded into my mind. As soon as the day broke, I rehearsed them as he spoke them to my companions, that they, as well as myself, might have something to say. And now, Socrates, to make an end my preface, I am ready to tell you the whole tale. I will give you not only the general heads, but the particulars, as they were told to me. The city and citizens, which you yesterday described to us in fiction, we will now transfer to the world of reality. It shall be the ancient city of Athens, and we will suppose that the citizens whom you imagined, were our veritable ancestors, of whom the priest spoke; they will perfectly harmonise, and there will be no inconsistency in saying that the citizens of your republic are these ancient Athenians. Let us divide the subject among us, and all endeavour according to our ability gracefully to execute the task which you have imposed upon us. Consider then, Socrates, if this narrative is suited to the purpose, or whether we should seek for some other instead.

Soc. And what other, Critias, can we find that will be better than this, which is natural and suitable to the festival of the goddess, and has the very great advantage of being a fact and not a fiction? How or where shall we find another if we abandon this? We cannot, *[27]* and therefore you must tell the tale, and good luck to you; and I in return for my yesterday's discourse will now rest and be a listener.

Crit. Let me proceed to explain to you, Socrates, the order in which we have arranged our entertainment. Our intention is, that Timaeus, who is the most of an astronomer amongst us, and has made the nature of the universe his special study, should speak first, beginning with the generation of the world and going down to the creation of man; next, I am to receive the men whom he has created of whom some will have profited by the excellent education which you have given them; and then, in accordance with the tale of Solon, and equally with his law, we will bring them into court and make them citizens, as if they were those very Athenians whom the sacred Egyptian record has recovered from oblivion, and thenceforward we will speak of them as Athenians and fellow-citizens.

Soc. I see that I shall receive in my turn a perfect and splendid feast of reason. And now, Timaeus, you, I suppose, should speak next, after duly calling upon the Gods.

Tim. All men, Socrates, who have any degree of right feeling, at the beginning of every enterprise, whether small or great, always call upon God. And we, too, who are going to discourse of the nature of the universe, how created or how existing without creation, if we be not altogether out of our wits, must invoke the aid of Gods and Goddesses and pray that our words may be acceptable to them and consistent with themselves. Let this, then, be our invocation of the Gods, to which I add an exhortation of myself to speak in such manner as will be most intelligible to you, and will most accord with my own intent.

First then, in my judgment, we must make a distinction and ask, What is that which always is and has no becoming; and what is that which is always becoming and never is? That which is apprehended by intelligence and reason is always in the same state; *[28]* but that which is conceived by opinion with the help of sensation and without reason, is always in a process of becoming and perishing and never really is. Now everything that becomes or is created must of necessity be created by some cause, for without a cause nothing can be created. The work of the creator, whenever he looks to the unchangeable and fashions the form and nature of his work after an unchangeable pattern, must necessarily be made fair and perfect; but when he looks to the created only, and uses a created pattern, it is not fair or perfect. Was the heaven then or the world, whether called by this or by any other more appropriate name-assuming the name, I am asking a question which has to be asked at the beginning of an enquiry about anything-was the world, I say, always in existence and without beginning? or created, and had it a beginning? Created, I reply, being visible and tangible and having a body, and therefore sensible; and all sensible things are apprehended by opinion and sense and are in a process of creation and created. Now that which is created must, as we affirm, of necessity be created by a cause. But the father and maker of all this universe is past finding out; and even if we found him, to tell of him to all men would be impossible. And there is still a question to be asked about him: Which of the patterns had the artificer in view when he made the world-the pattern of the unchangeable, or of that which is created? *[29]* If the world be indeed fair and the artificer good, it is manifest that he must have looked to that which is eternal; but if what cannot be said without blasphemy is true, then to the created pattern. Every one will see that he must have looked to, the eternal; for the world is the fairest of creations and he is the best of causes. And having been created in this way, the world has been framed in the likeness of that which is apprehended by reason and mind and is unchangeable, and must therefore of necessity, if this is admitted, be a copy of something. Now it is all-important that the beginning of everything should be according to nature. And in speaking of the copy and the original we may assume that words are akin to the matter which they describe; when they relate to the lasting and permanent and intelligible, they ought to be lasting and unalterable, and, as far as their nature allows, irrefutable and immovable-nothing less. But when they express only the copy or likeness and not the eternal things themselves, they need only be likely and analogous to the real words. As being is to becoming, so is truth to belief. If then, Socrates, amid the many opinions about the gods and the generation of the universe, we are not able to give notions which are altogether and in every respect exact and consistent with one another, do not be surprised. Enough, if we adduce probabilities as likely as any others; for we must remember that I who am the speaker, and you who are the judges, are only mortal men, and we ought to accept the tale which is probable and enquire no further.

Soc. Excellent, Timaeus; and we will do precisely as you bid us. The prelude is charming, and is already accepted by us-may we beg of you to proceed to the strain?

Tim. Let me tell you then why the creator made this world of generation. He was good, and the good can never have any jealousy of anything. And being free from jealousy, he desired that all things should be as like himself as they could be. This is in the truest sense the origin of creation and of the world, *[30]* as we shall do well in believing on the testimony of wise men: God desired that all things should be good and nothing bad, so far as this was attainable. Wherefore also finding the whole visible sphere not at rest, but moving in an irregular and disorderly fashion, out of disorder he brought order, considering that this was in every way better than the other. Now the deeds of the best could never be or have been other than the fairest; and the creator, reflecting on the things which are by nature visible, found that no unintelligent creature taken as a whole was fairer than the intelligent taken as a whole; and that intelligence could not be present in anything which was devoid of soul. For which reason, when he was framing the universe, he put intelligence in soul, and soul in body, that he might be the creator of a work which was by nature fairest and best. Wherefore, using the language of probability, we may say that the world became a living creature truly endowed with soul and intelligence by the providence of God.

This being supposed, let us proceed to the next stage: In the likeness of what animal did the Creator make the world? It would be an unworthy thing to liken it to any nature which exists as a part only; for nothing can be beautiful which is like any imperfect thing; but let us suppose the world to be the very image of that whole of which all other animals both individually and in their tribes are portions. For the original of the universe contains in itself all intelligible beings, just as this world comprehends us and all other visible creatures. For the Deity, intending to make this world like the fairest and most perfect of intelligible beings, framed one visible animal comprehending within itself all other animals of a kindred nature. *[31]* Are we right in saying that there is one world, or that they are many and infinite? There must be one only, if the created copy is to accord with the original. For that which includes all other intelligible creatures cannot have a second or companion; in that case there would be need of another living being which would include both, and of which they would be parts, and the likeness would be more truly said to resemble not them, but that other which included them. In order then that the world might be solitary, like the perfect animal, the creator made not two worlds or an infinite number of them; but there is and ever will be one only-begotten and created heaven.

Now that which is created is of necessity corporeal, and also visible and tangible. And nothing is visible where there is no fire, or tangible which has no solidity, and nothing is solid without earth. Wherefore also God in the beginning of creation made the body of the universe to consist of fire and earth. But two things cannot be rightly put together without a third; there must be some bond of union between them. And the fairest bond is that which makes the most complete fusion of itself and the things which it combines; and proportion is best adapted to effect such a union. For whenever in any three numbers, whether cube or square, there is a mean, which is to the last term what the first term is to it; *[32]* and again, when the mean is to the first term as the last term is to the mean-then the mean becoming first and last, and the first and last both becoming means, they will all of them of necessity come to be the same, and having become the same with one another will be all one. If the universal frame had been created a surface only and having no depth, a single mean would have sufficed to bind together itself and the other terms; but now, as the world must be solid, and solid bodies are always compacted not by one mean but by two, God placed water and air in the mean between fire and earth, and made them to have the same proportion so far as was possible (as fire is to air so is air to water, and as air is to water so is water to earth); and thus he bound and put together a visible and tangible heaven. And for these reasons, and out of such elements which are in number four, the body of the world was created, and it was harmonised by proportion, and therefore has the spirit of friendship; and having been reconciled to itself, it was indissoluble by the hand of any other than the framer.

Now the creation took up the whole of each of the four elements; for the Creator compounded the world out of all the fire and all the water and all the air and all the earth, leaving no part of any of them nor any power of them outside. His intention was, in the first place, that the animal should be as far as possible a perfect whole and of perfect parts: *[33]* secondly, that it should be one, leaving no remnants out of which another such world might be created: and also that it should be free from old age and unaffected by disease. Considering that if heat and cold and other powerful forces which unite bodies surround and attack them from without when they are unprepared, they decompose them, and by bringing diseases and old age upon them, make them waste away-for this cause and on these grounds he made the world one whole, having every part entire, and being therefore perfect and not liable to old age and disease. And he gave to the world the figure which was suitable and also natural. Now to the animal which was to comprehend all animals, that figure was suitable which comprehends within itself all other figures. Wherefore he made the world in the form of a globe, round as from a lathe, having its extremes in every direction equidistant from the centre, the most perfect and the most like itself of all figures; for he considered that the like is infinitely fairer than the unlike. This he finished off, making the surface smooth all around for many reasons; in the first place, because the living being had no need of eyes when there was nothing remaining outside him to be seen; nor of ears when there was nothing to be heard; and there was no surrounding atmosphere to be breathed; nor would there have been any use of organs by the help of which he might receive his food or get rid of what he had already digested, since there was nothing which went from him or came into him: for there was nothing beside him. Of design he was created thus, his own waste providing his own food, and all that he did or suffered taking place in and by himself. For the Creator conceived that a being which was self-sufficient would be far more excellent than one which lacked anything; and, as he had no need to take anything or defend himself against any one, the Creator did not think it necessary to bestow upon him hands: nor had he any need of feet, *[34]* nor of the whole apparatus of walking; but the movement suited to his spherical form was assigned to him, being of all the seven that which is most appropriate to mind and intelligence; and he was made to move in the same manner and on the same spot, within his own limits revolving in a circle. All the other six motions were taken away from him, and he was made not to partake of their deviations. And as this circular movement required no feet, the universe was created without legs and without feet.

Such was the whole plan of the eternal God about the god that was to be, to whom for this reason he gave a body, smooth and even, having a surface in every direction equidistant from the centre, a body entire and perfect, and formed out of perfect bodies. And in the centre he put the soul, which he diffused throughout the body, making it also to be the exterior environment of it; and he made the universe a circle moving in a circle, one and solitary, yet by reason of its excellence able to converse with itself, and needing no other friendship or acquaintance. Having these purposes in view he created the world a blessed god.

Now God did not make the soul after the body, although we are speaking of them in this order; for having brought them together he would never have allowed that the elder should be ruled by the younger; but this is a random manner of speaking which we have, because somehow we ourselves too are very much under the dominion of chance. Whereas he made the soul in origin and excellence prior to and older than the body, to be the ruler and mistress, of whom the body was to be the subject. And he made her out of the following elements and on this wise: *[35]* Out of the indivisible and unchangeable, and also out of that which is divisible and has to do with material bodies, he compounded a third and intermediate kind of essence, partaking of the nature of the same and of the other, and this compound he placed accordingly in a mean between the indivisible, and the divisible and material. He took the three elements of the same, the other, and the essence, and mingled them into one form, compressing by force the reluctant and unsociable nature of the other into the same. When he had mingled them with the essence and out of three made one, he again divided this whole into as many portions as was fitting, each portion being a compound of the same, the other, and the essence. And he proceeded to divide after this manner:-First of all, he took away one part of the whole [1], and then he separated a second part which was double the first [2], and then he took away a third part which was half as much again as the second and three times as much as the first [3], and then he took a fourth part which was twice as much as the second [4], and a fifth part which was three times the third [9], and a sixth part which was eight times the first [8], and a seventh part which was twenty-seven times the first [27]. After this he filled up the double intervals [i.e. between 1, 2, 4, 8] and *[36]* the triple [i.e. between 1, 3, 9, 27] cutting off yet other portions from the mixture and placing them in the intervals, so that in each interval there were two kinds of means, the one exceeding and exceeded by equal parts of its extremes [as for example 1, 4/3, 2, in which the mean 4/3 is one-third of 1 more than 1, and one-third of 2 less than 2], the other being that kind of mean which exceeds and is exceeded by an equal number. Where there were intervals of 3/2 and of 4/3 and of 9/8, made by the connecting terms in the former intervals, he filled up all the intervals of 4/3 with the interval of 9/8, leaving a fraction over; and the interval which this fraction expressed was in the ratio of 256 to 243. And thus the whole mixture out of which he cut these portions was all exhausted by him. This entire compound he divided lengthways into two parts, which he joined to one another at the centre like the letter X, and bent them into a circular form, connecting them with themselves and each other at the point opposite to their original meeting-point; and, comprehending them in a uniform revolution upon the same axis, he made the one the outer and the other the inner circle. Now the motion of the outer circle he called the motion of the same, and the motion of the inner circle the motion of the other or diverse. The motion of the same he carried round by the side to the right, and the motion of the diverse diagonally to the left. And he gave dominion to the motion of the same and like, for that he left single and undivided; but the inner motion he divided in six places and made seven unequal circles having their intervals in ratios of two-and three, three of each, and bade the orbits proceed in a direction opposite to one another; and three [Sun, Mercury, Venus] he made to move with equal swiftness, and the remaining four [Moon, Saturn, Mars, Jupiter] to move with unequal swiftness to the three and to one another, but in due proportion.

Now when the Creator had framed the soul according to his will, he formed within her the corporeal universe, and brought the two together, and united them centre to centre. The soul, interfused everywhere from the centre to the circumference of heaven, of which also she is the external envelopment, herself turning in herself, began a divine beginning of never ceasing and rational life enduring throughout all time. *[37]* The body of heaven is visible, but the soul is invisible, and partakes of reason and harmony, and being made by the best of intellectual and everlasting natures, is the best of things created. And because she is composed of the same and of the other and of the essence, these three, and is divided and united in due proportion, and in her revolutions returns upon herself, the soul, when touching anything which has essence, whether dispersed in parts or undivided, is stirred through all her powers, to declare the sameness or difference of that thing and some other; and to what individuals are related, and by what affected, and in what way and how and when, both in the world of generation and in the world of immutable being. And when reason, which works with equal truth, whether she be in the circle of the diverse or of the same-in voiceless silence holding her onward course in the sphere of the self-moved-when reason, I say, is hovering around the sensible world and when the circle of the diverse also moving truly imparts the intimations of sense to the whole soul, then arise opinions and beliefs sure and certain. But when reason is concerned with the rational, and the circle of the same moving smoothly declares it, then intelligence and knowledge are necessarily perfected. And if any one affirms that in which these two are found to be other than the soul, he will say the very opposite of the truth.

When the father creator saw the creature which he had made moving and living, the created image of the eternal gods, he rejoiced, and in his joy determined to make the copy still more like the original; and as this was eternal, he sought to make the universe eternal, so far as might be. Now the nature of the ideal being was everlasting, but to bestow this attribute in its fulness upon a creature was impossible. Wherefore he resolved to have a moving image of eternity, and when he set in order the heaven, he made this image eternal but moving according to number, while eternity itself rests in unity; and this image we call time. For there were no days and nights and months and years before the heaven was created, but when he constructed the heaven he created them also. They are all parts of time, and the past and future are created species of time, which we unconsciously but wrongly transfer to the eternal essence; for we say that he "was," he "is," he "will be," but the truth is that "is" alone is properly attributed to him, *[38]* and that "was" and "will be" only to be spoken of becoming in time, for they are motions, but that which is immovably the same cannot become older or younger by time, nor ever did or has become, or hereafter will be, older or younger, nor is subject at all to any of those states which affect moving and sensible things and of which generation is the cause. These are the forms of time, which imitates eternity and revolves according to a law of number. Moreover, when we say that what has become is become and what becomes is becoming, and that what will become is about to become and that the non-existent is non-existent-all these are inaccurate modes of expression. But perhaps this whole subject will be more suitably discussed on some other occasion.

Time, then, and the heaven came into being at the same instant in order that, having been created together, if ever there was to be a dissolution of them, they might be dissolved together. It was framed after the pattern of the eternal nature, that it might resemble this as far as was possible; for the pattern exists from eternity, and the created heaven has been, and is, and will be, in all time. Such was the mind and thought of God in the creation of time. The sun and moon and five other stars, which are called the planets, were created by him in order to distinguish and preserve the numbers of time; and when he had made-their several bodies, he placed them in the orbits in which the circle of the other was revolving-in seven orbits seven stars. First, there was the moon in the orbit nearest the earth, and next the sun, in the second orbit above the earth; then came the morning star and the star sacred to Hermes, moving in orbits which have an equal swiftness with the sun, but in an opposite direction; and this is the reason why the sun and Hermes and Lucifer overtake and are overtaken by each other. To enumerate the places which he assigned to the other stars, and to give all the reasons why he assigned them, although a secondary matter, would give more trouble than the primary. These things at some future time, when we are at leisure, may have the consideration which they deserve, but not at present.

Now, when all the stars which were necessary to the creation of time had attained a motion suitable to them,-and had become living creatures having bodies fastened by vital chains, and learnt their appointed task, *[39]* moving in the motion of the diverse, which is diagonal, and passes through and is governed by the motion of the same, they revolved, some in a larger and some in a lesser orbit-those which had the lesser orbit revolving faster, and those which had the larger more slowly. Now by reason of the motion of the same, those which revolved fastest appeared to be overtaken by those which moved slower although they really overtook them; for the motion of the same made them all turn in a spiral, and, because some went one way and some another, that which receded most slowly from the sphere of the same, which was the swiftest, appeared to follow it most nearly. That there might be some visible measure of their relative swiftness and slowness as they proceeded in their eight courses, God lighted a fire, which we now call the sun, in the second from the earth of these orbits, that it might give light to the whole of heaven, and that the animals, as many as nature intended, might participate in number, learning arithmetic from the revolution of the same and the like. Thus then, and for this reason the night and the day were created, being the period of the one most intelligent revolution. And the month is accomplished when the moon has completed her orbit and overtaken the sun, and the year when the sun has completed his own orbit. Mankind, with hardly an exception, have not remarked the periods of the other stars, and they have no name for them, and do not measure them against one another by the help of number, and hence they can scarcely be said to know that their wanderings, being infinite in number and admirable for their variety, make up time. And yet there is no difficulty in seeing that the perfect number of time fulfils the perfect year when all the eight revolutions, having their relative degrees of swiftness, are accomplished together and attain their completion at the same time, measured by the rotation of the same and equally moving. After this manner, and for these reasons, came into being such of the stars as in their heavenly progress received reversals of motion, to the end that the created heaven might imitate the eternal nature, and be as like as possible to the perfect and intelligible animal.

Thus far and until the birth of time the created universe was made in the likeness of the original, but inasmuch as all animals were not yet comprehended therein, it was still unlike. What remained, the creator then proceeded to fashion after the nature of the pattern. Now as in the ideal animal the mind perceives ideas or species of a certain nature and number, he thought that this created animal ought to have species of a like nature and number. There are four such; *[40]* one of them is the heavenly race of the gods; another, the race of birds whose way is in the air; the third, the watery species; and the fourth, the pedestrian and land creatures. Of the heavenly and divine, he created the greater part out of fire, that they might be the brightest of all things and fairest to behold, and he fashioned them after the likeness of the universe in the figure of a circle, and made them follow the intelligent motion of the supreme, distributing them over the whole circumference of heaven, which was to be a true cosmos or glorious world spangled with them all over. And he gave to each of them two movements: the first, a movement on the same spot after the same manner, whereby they ever continue to think consistently the same thoughts about the same things; the second, a forward movement, in which they are controlled by the revolution of the same and the like; but by the other five motions they were unaffected, in order that each of them might attain the highest perfection. And for this reason the fixed stars were created, to be divine and eternal animals, ever-abiding and revolving after the same manner and on the same spot; and the other stars which reverse their motion and are subject to deviations of this kind, were created in the manner already described. The earth, which is our nurse, clinging around the pole which is extended through the universe, he framed to be the guardian and artificer of night and day, first and eldest of gods that are in the interior of heaven. Vain would be the attempt to tell all the figures of them circling as in dance, and their juxtapositions, and the return of them in their revolutions upon themselves, and their approximations, and to say which of these deities in their conjunctions meet, and which of them are in opposition, and in what order they get behind and before one another, and when they are severally eclipsed to our sight and again reappear, sending terrors and intimations of the future to those who cannot calculate their movements-to attempt to tell of all this without a visible representation of the heavenly system would be labour in vain. Enough on this head; and now let what we have said about the nature of the created and visible gods have an end.

To know or tell the origin of the other divinities is beyond us, and we must accept the traditions of the men of old time who affirm themselves to be the offspring of the gods-that is what they say-and they must surely have known their own ancestors. How can we doubt the word of the children of the gods? Although they give no probable or certain proofs, still, as they declare that they are speaking of what took place in their own family, we must conform to custom and believe them. In this manner, then, according to them, the genealogy of these gods is to be received and set forth.

Oceanus and Tethys were the children of Earth and Heaven, and from these sprang Phorcys and Cronos and Rhea, and all that generation; *[41]* and from Cronos and Rhea sprang Zeus and Here, and all those who are said to be their brethren, and others who were the children of these.

Now, when all of them, both those who visibly appear in their revolutions as well as those other gods who are of a more retiring nature, had come into being, the creator of the universe addressed them in these words: "Gods, children of gods, who are my works, and of whom I am the artificer and father, my creations are indissoluble, if so I will. All that is bound may be undone, but only an evil being would wish to undo that which is harmonious and happy. Wherefore, since ye are but creatures, ye are not altogether immortal and indissoluble, but ye shall certainly not be dissolved, nor be liable to the fate of death, having in my will a greater and mightier bond than those with which ye were bound at the time of your birth. And now listen to my instructions:-Three tribes of mortal beings remain to be created-without them the universe will be incomplete, for it will not contain every kind of animal which it ought to contain, if it is to be perfect. On the other hand, if they were created by me and received life at my hands, they would be on an equality with the gods. In order then that they may be mortal, and that this universe may be truly universal, do ye, according to your natures, betake yourselves to the formation of animals, imitating the power which was shown by me in creating you. The part of them worthy of the name immortal, which is called divine and is the guiding principle of those who are willing to follow justice and you-of that divine part I will myself sow the seed, and having made a beginning, I will hand the work over to you. And do ye then interweave the mortal with the immortal, and make and beget living creatures, and give them food, and make them to grow, and receive them again in death."

Thus he spake, and once more into the cup in which he had previously mingled the soul of the universe he poured the remains of the elements, and mingled them in much the same manner; they were not, however, pure as before, but diluted to the second and third degree. And having made it he divided the whole mixture into souls equal in number to the stars, and assigned each soul to a star; and having there placed them as in a chariot, he showed them the nature of the universe, and declared to them the laws of destiny, according to which their first birth would be one and the same for all,-no one should suffer a disadvantage at his hands; they were to be sown in the instruments of time severally adapted to them, *[42]* and to come forth the most religious of animals; and as human nature was of two kinds, the superior race would here after be called man. Now, when they should be implanted in bodies by necessity, and be always gaining or losing some part of their bodily substance, then in the first place it would be necessary that they should all have in them one and the same faculty of sensation, arising out of irresistible impressions; in the second place, they must have love, in which pleasure and pain mingle; also fear and anger, and the feelings which are akin or opposite to them; if they conquered these they would live righteously, and if they were conquered by them, unrighteously. He who lived well during his appointed time was to return and dwell in his native star, and there he would have a blessed and congenial existence. But if he failed in attaining this, at the second birth he would pass into a woman, and if, when in that state of being, he did not desist from evil, he would continually be changed into some brute who resembled him in the evil nature which he had acquired, and would not cease from his toils and transformations until he followed the revolution of the same and the like within him, and overcame by the help of reason the turbulent and irrational mob of later accretions, made up of fire and air and water and earth, and returned to the form of his first and better state. Having given all these laws to his creatures, that he might be guiltless of future evil in any of them, the creator sowed some of them in the earth, and some in the moon, and some in the other instruments of time; and when he had sown them he committed to the younger gods the fashioning of their mortal bodies, and desired them to furnish what was still lacking to the human soul, and having made all the suitable additions, to rule over them, and to pilot the mortal animal in the best and wisest manner which they could, and avert from him all but self-inflicted evils.

When the creator had made all these ordinances he remained in his own accustomed nature, and his children heard and were obedient to their father's word, and receiving from him the immortal principle of a mortal creature, in imitation of their own creator they borrowed portions of fire, and earth, and water, and air from the world, *[43]* which were hereafter to be restored-these they took and welded them together, not with the indissoluble chains by which they were themselves bound, but with little pegs too small to be visible, making up out of all the four elements each separate body, and fastening the courses of the immortal soul in a body which was in a state of perpetual influx and efflux. Now these courses, detained as in a vast river, neither overcame nor were overcome; but were hurrying and hurried to and fro, so that the whole animal was moved and progressed, irregularly however and irrationally and anyhow, in all the six directions of motion, wandering backwards and forwards, and right and left, and up and down, and in all the six directions. For great as was the advancing and retiring flood which provided nourishment, the affections produced by external contact caused still greater tumult-when the body of any one met and came into collision with some external fire, or with the solid earth or the gliding waters, or was caught in the tempest borne on the air, and the motions produced by any of these impulses were carried through the body to the soul. All such motions have consequently received the general name of "sensations," which they still retain. And they did in fact at that time create a very great and mighty movement; uniting with the ever flowing stream in stirring up and violently shaking the courses of the soul, they completely stopped the revolution of the same by their opposing current, and hindered it from predominating and advancing; and they so disturbed the nature of the other or diverse, that the three double intervals [i.e. between 1, 2, 4, 8], and the three triple intervals [i.e. between 1, 3, 9, 27], together with the mean terms and connecting links which are expressed by the ratios of 3 : 2, and 4 : 3, and of 9 : 8-these, although they cannot be wholly undone except by him who united them, were twisted by them in all sorts of ways, and the circles were broken and disordered in every possible manner, so that when they moved they were tumbling to pieces, and moved irrationally, at one time in a reverse direction, and then again obliquely, and then upside down, as you might imagine a person who is upside down and has his head leaning upon the ground and his feet up against something in the air; and when he is in such a position, both he and the spectator fancy that the right of either is his left, and left right. If, when powerfully experiencing these and similar effects, the revolutions of the soul come in contact with some external thing, *[44]* either of the class of the same or of the other, they speak of the same or of the other in a manner the very opposite of the truth; and they become false and foolish, and there is no course or revolution in them which has a guiding or directing power; and if again any sensations enter in violently from without and drag after them the whole vessel of the soul, then the courses of the soul, though they seem to conquer, are really conquered.

And by reason of all these affections, the soul, when encased in a mortal body, now, as in the beginning, is at first without intelligence; but when the flood of growth and nutriment abates, and the courses of the soul, calming down, go their own way and become steadier as time goes on, then the several circles return to their natural form, and their revolutions are corrected, and they call the same and the other by their right names, and make the possessor of them to become a rational being. And if these combine in him with any true nurture or education, he attains the fulness and health of the perfect man, and escapes the worst disease of all; but if he neglects education he walks lame to the end of his life, and returns imperfect and good for nothing to the world below. This, however, is a later stage; at present we must treat more exactly the subject before us, which involves a preliminary enquiry into the generation of the body and its members, and as to how the soul was created-for what reason and by what providence of the gods; and holding fast to probability, we must pursue our way.

First, then, the gods, imitating the spherical shape of the universe, enclosed the two divine courses in a spherical body, that, namely, which we now term the head, being the most divine part of us and the lord of all that is in us: to this the gods, when they put together the body, gave all the other members to be servants, considering that it partook of every sort of motion. In order then that it might not tumble about among the high and deep places of the earth, but might be able to get over the one and out of the other, they provided the body to be its vehicle and means of locomotion; which consequently had length and was furnished with four limbs extended and flexible; these God contrived to be instruments of locomotion with which it might take hold and find support, *[45]* and so be able to pass through all places, carrying on high the dwelling-place of the most sacred and divine part of us. Such was the origin of legs and hands, which for this reason were attached to every man; and the gods, deeming the front part of man to be more honourable and more fit to command than the hinder part, made us to move mostly in a forward direction. Wherefore man must needs have his front part unlike and distinguished from the rest of his body.

And so in the vessel of the head, they first of all put a face in which they inserted organs to minister in all things to the providence of the soul, and they appointed this part, which has authority, to be by nature the part which is in front. And of the organs they first contrived the eyes to give light, and the principle according to which they were inserted was as follows: So much of fire as would not burn, but gave a gentle light, they formed into a substance akin to the light of every-day life; and the pure fire which is within us and related thereto they made to flow through the eyes in a stream smooth and dense, compressing the whole eye, and especially the centre part, so that it kept out everything of a coarser nature, and allowed to pass only this pure element. When the light of day surrounds the stream of vision, then like falls upon like, and they coalesce, and one body is formed by natural affinity in the line of vision, wherever the light that falls from within meets with an external object. And the whole stream of vision, being similarly affected in virtue of similarity, diffuses the motions of what it touches or what touches it over the whole body, until they reach the soul, causing that perception which we call sight. But when night comes on and the external and kindred fire departs, then the stream of vision is cut off; for going forth to an unlike element it is changed and extinguished, being no longer of one nature with the surrounding atmosphere which is now deprived of fire: and so the eye no longer sees, and we feel disposed to sleep. For when the eyelids, which the gods invented for the preservation of sight, are closed, they keep in the internal fire; and the power of the fire diffuses and equalises the inward motions; when they are equalised, there is rest, and when the rest is profound, *[46]* sleep comes over us scarce disturbed by dreams; but where the greater motions still remain, of whatever nature and in whatever locality, they engender corresponding visions in dreams, which are remembered by us when we are awake and in the external world. And now there is no longer any difficulty in understanding the creation of images in mirrors and all smooth and bright surfaces. For from the communion of the internal and external fires, and again from the union of them and their numerous transformations when they meet in the mirror, all these appearances of necessity arise, when the fire from the face coalesces with the fire from the eye on the bright and smooth surface. And right appears left and left right, because the visual rays come into contact with the rays emitted by the object in a manner contrary to the usual mode of meeting; but the right appears right, and the left left, when the position of one of the two concurring lights is reversed; and this happens when the mirror is concave and its smooth surface repels the right stream of vision to the left side, and the left to the right. Or if the mirror be turned vertically, then the concavity makes the countenance appear to be all upside down, and the lower rays are driven upwards and the upper downwards.

All these are to be reckoned among the second and co-operative causes which God, carrying into execution the idea of the best as far as possible, uses as his ministers. They are thought by most men not to be the second, but the prime causes of all things, because they freeze and heat, and contract and dilate, and the like. But they are not so, for they are incapable of reason or intellect; the only being which can properly have mind is the invisible soul, whereas fire and water, and earth and air, are all of them visible bodies. The lover of intellect and knowledge ought to explore causes of intelligent nature first of all, and, secondly, of those things which, being moved by others, are compelled to move others. And this is what we too must do. Both kinds of causes should be acknowledged by us, but a distinction should be made between those which are endowed with mind and are the workers of things fair and good, and those which are deprived of intelligence and always produce chance effects without order or design. Of the second or co-operative causes of sight, which help to give to the eyes the power which they now possess, enough has been said. I will therefore now proceed to speak of the higher use and purpose for which God has given them to us. *[47]* The sight in my opinion is the source of the greatest benefit to us, for had we never seen the stars, and the sun, and the heaven, none of the words which we have spoken about the universe would ever have been uttered. But now the sight of day and night, and the months and the revolutions of the years, have created number, and have given us a conception of time, and the power of enquiring about the nature of the universe; and from this source we have derived philosophy, than which no greater good ever was or will be given by the gods to mortal man. This is the greatest boon of sight: and of the lesser benefits why should I speak? even the ordinary man if he were deprived of them would bewail his loss, but in vain. Thus much let me say however: God invented and gave us sight to the end that we might behold the courses of intelligence in the heaven, and apply them to the courses of our own intelligence which are akin to them, the unperturbed to the perturbed; and that we, learning them and partaking of the natural truth of reason, might imitate the absolutely unerring courses of God and regulate our own vagaries. The same may be affirmed of speech and hearing: they have been given by the gods to the same end and for a like reason. For this is the principal end of speech, whereto it most contributes. Moreover, so much of music as is adapted to the sound of the voice and to the sense of hearing is granted to us for the sake of harmony; and harmony, which has motions akin to the revolutions of our souls, is not regarded by the intelligent votary of the Muses as given by them with a view to irrational pleasure, which is deemed to be the purpose of it in our day, but as meant to correct any discord which may have arisen in the courses of the soul, and to be our ally in bringing her into harmony and agreement with herself; and rhythm too was given by them for the same reason, on account of the irregular and graceless ways which prevail among mankind generally, and to help us against them.

Thus far in what we have been saying, with small exception, the works of intelligence have been set forth; and now we must place by the side of them in our discourse the things which come into being through necessity-for the creation is mixed, *[48]* being made up of necessity and mind. Mind, the ruling power, persuaded necessity to bring the greater part of created things to perfection, and thus and after this manner in the beginning, when the influence of reason got the better of necessity, the universe was created. But if a person will truly tell of the way in which the work was accomplished, he must include the other influence of the variable cause as well. Wherefore, we must return again and find another suitable beginning, as about the former matters, so also about these. To which end we must consider the nature of fire, and water, and air, and earth, such as they were prior to the creation of the heaven, and what was happening to them in this previous state; for no one has as yet explained the manner of their generation, but we speak of fire and the rest of them, whatever they mean, as though men knew their natures, and we maintain them to be the first principles and letters or elements of the whole, when they cannot reasonably be compared by a man of any sense even to syllables or first compounds. And let me say thus much: I will not now speak of the first principle or principles of all things, or by whatever name they are to be called, for this reason-because it is difficult to set forth my opinion according to the method of discussion which we are at present employing. Do not imagine, any more than I can bring myself to imagine, that I should be right in undertaking so great and difficult a task. Remembering what I said at first about probability, I will do my best to give as probable an explanation as any other-or rather, more probable; and I will first go back to the beginning and try to speak of each thing and of all. Once more, then, at the commencement of my discourse, I call upon God, and beg him to be our saviour out of a strange and unwonted enquiry, and to bring us to the haven of probability. So now let us begin again.

This new beginning of our discussion of the universe requires a fuller division than the former; for then we made two classes, now a third must be revealed. The two sufficed for the former discussion: one, which we assumed, was a pattern intelligible and always the same; *[49]* and the second was only the imitation of the pattern, generated and visible. There is also a third kind which we did not distinguish at the time, conceiving that the two would be enough. But now the argument seems to require that we should set forth in words another kind, which is difficult of explanation and dimly seen. What nature are we to attribute to this new kind of being? We reply, that it is the receptacle, and in a manner the nurse, of all generation. I have spoken the truth; but I must express myself in clearer language, and this will be an arduous task for many reasons, and in particular because I must first raise questions concerning fire and the other elements, and determine what each of them is; for to say, with any probability or certitude, which of them should be called water rather than fire, and which should be called any of them rather than all or some one of them, is a difficult matter. How, then, shall we settle this point, and what questions about the elements may be fairly raised?

In the first place, we see that what we just now called water, by condensation, I suppose, becomes stone and earth; and this same element, when melted and dispersed, passes into vapour and air. Air, again, when inflamed, becomes fire; and again fire, when condensed and extinguished, passes once more into the form of air; and once more, air, when collected and condensed, produces cloud and mist; and from these, when still more compressed, comes flowing water, and from water comes earth and stones once more; and thus generation appears to be transmitted from one to the other in a circle. Thus, then, as the several elements never present themselves in the same form, how can any one have the assurance to assert positively that any of them, whatever it may be, is one thing rather than another? No one can. But much the safest plan is to speak of them as follows:-Anything which we see to be continually changing, as, for example, fire, we must not call "this" or "that," but rather say that it is "of such a nature"; nor let us speak of water as "this"; but always as "such"; nor must we imply that there is any stability in any of those things which we indicate by the use of the words "this" and "that," supposing ourselves to signify something thereby; for they are too volatile to be detained in any such expressions as "this," or "that," or "relative to this," or any other mode of speaking which represents them as permanent. We ought not to apply "this" to any of them, but rather the word "such"; which expresses the similar principle circulating in each and all of them; for example, that should be called "fire" which is of such a nature always, and so of everything that has generation. That in which the elements severally grow up, and appear, and decay, is alone to be called by the name "this" or "that"; *[50]* but that which is of a certain nature, hot or white, or anything which admits of opposite equalities, and all things that are compounded of them, ought not to be so denominated. Let me make another attempt to explain my meaning more clearly. Suppose a person to make all kinds of figures of gold and to be always transmuting one form into all the rest-somebody points to one of them and asks what it is. By far the safest and truest answer is, That is gold; and not to call the triangle or any other figures which are formed in the gold "these," as though they had existence, since they are in process of change while he is making the assertion; but if the questioner be willing to take the safe and indefinite expression, "such," we should be satisfied. And the same argument applies to the universal nature which receives all bodies-that must be always called the same; for, while receiving all things, she never departs at all from her own nature, and never in any way, or at any time, assumes a form like that of any of the things which enter into her; she is the natural recipient of all impressions, and is stirred and informed by them, and appears different from time to time by reason of them. But the forms which enter into and go out of her are the likenesses of real existences modelled after their patterns in wonderful and inexplicable manner, which we will hereafter investigate. For the present we have only to conceive of three natures: first, that which is in process of generation; secondly, that in which the generation takes place; and thirdly, that of which the thing generated is a resemblance. And we may liken the receiving principle to a mother, and the source or spring to a father, and the intermediate nature to a child; and may remark further, that if the model is to take every variety of form, then the matter in which the model is fashioned will not be duly prepared, unless it is formless, and free from the impress of any of these shapes which it is hereafter to receive from without. For if the matter

121

were like any of the supervening forms, then whenever any opposite or entirely different nature was stamped upon its surface, it would take the impression badly, because it would intrude its own shape. Wherefore, that which is to receive all forms should have no form; as in making perfumes they first contrive that the liquid substance which is to receive the scent shall be as inodorous as possible; or as those who wish to impress figures on soft substances do not allow any previous impression to remain, *[51]* but begin by making the surface as even and smooth as possible. In the same way that which is to receive perpetually and through its whole extent the resemblances of all eternal beings ought to be devoid of any particular form. Wherefore, the mother and receptacle of all created and visible and in any way sensible things, is not to be termed earth, or air, or fire, or water, or any of their compounds or any of the elements from which these are derived, but is an invisible and formless being which receives all things and in some mysterious way partakes of the intelligible, and is most incomprehensible. In saying this we shall not be far wrong; as far, however, as we can attain to a knowledge of her from the previous considerations, we may truly say that fire is that part of her nature which from time to time is inflamed, and water that which is moistened, and that the mother substance becomes earth and air, in so far as she receives the impressions of them.

Let us consider this question more precisely. Is there any self-existent fire? and do all those things which we call self-existent exist? or are only those things which we see, or in some way perceive through the bodily organs, truly existent, and nothing whatever besides them? And is all that which, we call an intelligible essence nothing at all, and only a name? Here is a question which we must not leave unexamined or undetermined, nor must we affirm too confidently that there can be no decision; neither must we interpolate in our present long discourse a digression equally long, but if it is possible to set forth a great principle in a few words, that is just what we want.

Thus I state my view:-If mind and true opinion are two distinct classes, then I say that there certainly are these self-existent ideas unperceived by sense, and apprehended only by the mind; if, however, as some say, true opinion differs in no respect from mind, then everything that we perceive through the body is to be regarded as most real and certain. But we must affirm that to be distinct, for they have a distinct origin and are of a different nature; the one is implanted in us by instruction, the other by persuasion; the one is always accompanied by true reason, the other is without reason; the one cannot be overcome by persuasion, but the other can: and lastly, every man may be said to share in true opinion, but mind is the attribute of the gods and of very few men. Wherefore also we must acknowledge that there is one kind of being which is always the same, *[52]* uncreated and indestructible, never receiving anything into itself from without, nor itself going out to any other, but invisible and imperceptible by any sense, and of which the contemplation is granted to intelligence only. And there is another nature of the same name with it, and like to it, perceived by sense, created, always in motion, becoming in place and again vanishing out of place, which is apprehended by opinion and sense. And there is a third nature, which is space, and is eternal, and admits not of destruction and provides a home for all created things, and is apprehended without the help of sense, by a kind of spurious reason, and is hardly real; which we beholding as in a dream, say of all existence that it must of necessity be in some place and occupy a space, but that what is neither in heaven nor in earth has no existence. Of these and other things of the same kind, relating to the true and waking reality of nature, we have only this dreamlike sense, and we are unable to cast off sleep and determine the truth about them. For an image, since the reality, after which it is modelled, does not belong to it, and it exists ever as the fleeting shadow of some other, must be inferred to be in another [i.e. in space], grasping existence in some way or other, or it could not be at all. But true and exact reason, vindicating the nature of true being, maintains that while two things [i.e. the image and space] are different they cannot exist one of them in the other and so be one and also two at the same time.

Thus have I concisely given the result of my thoughts; and my verdict is that being and space and generation, these three, existed in their three ways before the heaven; and that the nurse of generation, moistened by water and inflamed by fire, and receiving the forms of earth and air, and experiencing all the affections which accompany these, presented a strange variety of appearances; and being full of powers which were neither similar nor equally balanced, was never in any part in a state of equipoise, but swaying unevenly hither and thither, was shaken by them, and by its motion again shook them; and the elements when moved were separated and carried continually, some one way, some another; as, when rain is shaken and winnowed by fans and other instruments used in the threshing of corn, *[53]* the close and heavy particles are borne away and settle in one direction, and the loose and light particles in another. In this manner, the four kinds or elements were then shaken by the receiving vessel, which, moving like a winnowing machine, scattered far away from one another the elements most unlike, and forced the most similar elements into dose contact. Wherefore also the various elements had different places before they were arranged so as to form the universe. At first, they were all without reason and measure. But when the world began to get into order, fire and water and earth and air had only certain faint traces of themselves, and were altogether such as everything might be expected to be in the absence of God; this, I say, was their nature at that time, and God fashioned them by form and number. Let it be consistently maintained by us in all that we say that God made them as far as possible the fairest and best, out of things which were not fair and good. And now I will endeavour to show you the disposition and generation of them by an unaccustomed argument, which am compelled to use; but I believe that you will be able to follow me, for your education has made you familiar with the methods of science.

In the first place, then, as is evident to all, fire and earth and water and air are bodies. And every sort of body possesses solidity, and every solid must necessarily be contained in planes; and every plane rectilinear figure is composed of triangles; and all triangles are originally of two kinds, both of which are made up of one right and two acute angles; one of them has at either end of the base the half of a divided right angle, having equal sides, while in the other the right angle is divided into unequal parts, having unequal sides. These, then, proceeding by a combination of probability with demonstration, we assume to be the original elements of fire and the other bodies; but the principles which are prior to these God only knows, and he of men who is the friend God. And next we have to determine what are the four most beautiful bodies which are unlike one another, and of which some are capable of resolution into one another; for having discovered thus much, we shall know the true origin of earth and fire and of the proportionate and intermediate elements. And then we shall not be willing to allow that there are any distinct kinds of visible bodies fairer than these. Wherefore we must endeavour to construct the four forms of bodies which excel in beauty, and then we shall be able to say that we have sufficiently apprehended their nature. *[54]* Now of the two triangles, the isosceles has one form only; the scalene or unequal-sided has an infinite number. Of the infinite forms we must select the most beautiful, if we are to proceed in due order, and any one who can point out a more beautiful form than ours for the construction of these bodies, shall carry off the palm, not as an enemy, but as a friend. Now, the one which we maintain to be the most beautiful of all the many triangles (and we need not speak of the others) is that of which the double forms a third triangle which is equilateral; the reason of this would be long to tell; he who disproves what we are saying, and shows that we are mistaken, may claim a friendly victory. Then let us choose two triangles, out of which fire and the other elements have been constructed, one isosceles, the other having the square of the longer side equal to three times the square of the lesser side.

Now is the time to explain what was before obscurely said: there was an error in imagining that all the four elements might be generated by and into one another; this, I say, was an erroneous supposition, for there are generated from the triangles which we have selected four kinds-three from the one which has the sides unequal; the fourth alone is framed out of the isosceles triangle. Hence they cannot all be resolved into one another, a great number of small bodies being combined into a few large ones, or the converse. But three of them can be thus resolved and compounded, for they all spring from one, and when the greater bodies are broken up, many small bodies will spring up out of them and take their own proper figures; or, again, when many small bodies are dissolved into their triangles, if they become one, they will form one large mass of another kind. So much for their passage into one another. I have now to speak of their several kinds, and show out of what combinations of numbers each of them was formed. The first will be the simplest and smallest construction, and its element is that triangle which has its hypotenuse twice the lesser side. When two such triangles are joined at the diagonal, and this is repeated three times, and the triangles rest their diagonals and shorter sides on the same point as a centre, a single equilateral triangle is formed out of six triangles; and four equilateral triangles, if put together, make out of every three plane angles one solid angle, being that which is nearest to the most obtuse of plane angles; *[55]* and out of the combination of these four angles arises the first solid form which distributes into equal and similar parts the whole circle in which it is inscribed. The second species of solid is formed out of the same triangles, which unite as eight equilateral triangles and form one solid angle out of four plane angles, and out of six such angles the second body is completed. And the third body is made up of 120 triangular elements, forming twelve solid angles, each of them included in five plane equilateral triangles, having altogether twenty bases, each of which is an equilateral triangle. The one element [that is, the triangle which has its hypotenuse twice the lesser side] having generated these figures, generated no more; but the isosceles triangle produced the fourth elementary figure, which is compounded of four such triangles, joining their right angles in a centre, and forming one equilateral quadrangle. Six of these united form eight solid angles, each of which is made by the combination of three plane right angles; the figure of the body thus composed is a cube, having six plane quadrangular equilateral bases. There was yet a fifth combination which God used in the delineation of the universe.

Now, he who, duly reflecting on all this, enquires whether the worlds are to be regarded as indefinite or definite in number, will be of opinion that the notion of their indefiniteness is characteristic of a sadly indefinite and ignorant mind. He, however, who raises the question whether they are to be truly regarded as one or five, takes up a more reasonable position. Arguing from probabilities, I am of opinion that they are one; another, regarding the question from another point of view, will be of another mind. But, leaving this enquiry, let us proceed to distribute the elementary forms, which have now been created in idea, among the four elements.

To earth, then, let us assign the cubical form; for earth is the most immoveable of the four and the most plastic of all bodies, and that which has the most stable bases must of necessity be of such a nature. Now, of the triangles which we assumed at first, that which has two equal sides is by nature more firmly based than that which has unequal sides; and of the compound figures which are formed out of either, the plane equilateral quadrangle has necessarily, a more stable basis than the equilateral triangle, both in the whole and in the parts. *[56]* Wherefore, in assigning this figure to earth, we adhere to probability; and to water we assign that one of the remaining forms which is the least moveable; and the most moveable of them to fire; and to air that which is intermediate. Also we assign the smallest body to fire, and the greatest to water, and the intermediate in size to air; and, again, the acutest body to fire, and the next in acuteness to, air, and the third to water. Of all these elements, that which has the fewest bases must necessarily be the most moveable, for it must be the acutest and most penetrating in every way, and also the lightest as being composed of the smallest number of similar particles: and the second body has similar properties in a second degree, and the third body in the third degree. Let it be agreed, then, both according to strict reason and according to probability, that the pyramid is the solid which is the original element and seed of fire; and let us assign the element which was next in the order of generation to air, and the third to water. We must imagine all these to be so small that no single particle of any of the four kinds is seen by us on account of their smallness: but when many of them are collected together their aggregates are seen. And the ratios of their numbers, motions, and other properties, everywhere God, as far as necessity allowed or gave consent, has exactly perfected, and harmonised in due proportion.

From all that we have just been saying about the elements or kinds, the most probable conclusion is as follows: â€" earth, when meeting with fire and dissolved by its sharpness, whether the dissolution take place in the fire itself or perhaps in some mass of air or water, is borne hither and thither, until its parts, meeting together and mutually harmonising, again become earth; for they can never take any other form. But water, when divided by fire or by air, on reforming, may become one part fire and two parts ai ; and a single volume of air divided becomes two of fire. Again, when a small body of fire is contained in a larger body of air or water or earth, and both are moving, and the fire struggling is overcome and broken up, then two volumes of fire form one volume of air; and when air is overcome and cut up into small pieces, two and a half parts of air are condensed into one part of water. Let us consider the matter in another way. When one of the other elements is fastened upon by fire, *[57]* and is cut by the sharpness of its angles and sides, it coalesces with the fire, and then ceases to be cut by them any longer. For no element which is one and the same with itself can be changed by or change another of the same kind and in the same state. But so long as in the process of transition the weaker is fighting against the stronger, the dissolution continues. Again, when a few small particles, enclosed in many larger ones, are in process of decomposition and extinction, they only cease from their tendency to extinction when they consent to pass into the conquering nature, and fire becomes air and air water. But if bodies of another kind go and attack them [i.e. the small particles], the latter continue to be dissolved until, being completely forced back and dispersed, they make their escape to their own kindred, or else, being overcome and assimilated to the conquering power, they remain where they are and dwell with their victors, and from being many become one. And owing to these affections, all things are changing their place, for by the motion of the receiving vessel the bulk of each class is distributed into its proper place; but those things which become unlike themselves and like other things, are hurried by the shaking into the place of the things to which they grow like.

(a) Fibonacci series numbers with arithmetic differences between numbers.	(b) Numbers in column (a) multiplied by a species of the golden ratio (phi): .61803 (1/1.61803 = .61803).	(c) Number from column (b) added to the number that was subtracted in column (a).	(d) The sum derived from the two numbers added in column (c). (This is the Lucas series, an arithmetic series, where every number is the sum of the two numbers preceding.)	(e) Each number from column (d) is a power of phi. Also, each number from column (d) is the phi number between two successive numbers from the Fibonacci series.	(f) Each Lucas number from column (d) is the approximate sum of the two non-consecutive, Fibonacci numbers preceding it from column (a) (ex: 11.09 ≈ 3 + 8 = 11)
3 − 2 = 1	.61803 x 1 = .61803	.61803 + 2	2.61803	phi^2	2.61803 ≈ 0 + 2
5 − 3 = 2	.61803 x 2 = 1.2306	1.23606 + 3	4.236	phi^3	4.236 ≈ 1 + 3
8 − 5 = 3	.61803 x 3 = 1.85409	1.85409 + 5	6.854	phi^4	6.854 ≈ 2 + 5
13 − 8 = 5	.61803 x 5 = 3.09015	3.09015 + 8	11.09	phi^5	11.090 ≈ 3 + 8
21 − 13 = 8	.61803 x 8 = 4.94424	4.94424 + 13	17.944	phi^6	17.944 ≈ 5 + 13
34 − 21 = 13	.61803 x 13 = 8.03439	8.03439 + 21	29.034	phi^7	29.03 ≈ 8 + 21
55 − 34 = 21	.61803 x 21 = 12.97863	12.97863 + 34	46.978	phi^8	46.97 ≈ 13 + 34
89 − 55 = 34	.61803 x 34 = 21.01302	21.01302 + 55	76.013	phi^9	76.013 ≈ 21 + 55
144 − 89 = 55	.61803 x 55 = 33.99165	33.99165 + 89	122.99	phi^{10}	122.99 ≈ 34 + 89
233 − 144 = 89	.61803 x 89 = 55.00467	55.00467 + 144	199.004	phi^{11}	199.004 ≈ 55 + 144
377 − 233 = 144	.61803 x 144 = 88.99	88.992 + 233	321.992	phi^{12}	321.99 ≈ 89 + 233

The golden ratio (phi), and Fibonacci[62] and Lucas[63] numbers

[62] Wikipedia, "Fibonacci Number" Fibonacci number - Wikipedia accessed April 12, 2021

[63] Wikipedia, "Lucas Number" Lucas number - Wikipedia accessed April 12, 2021

Appendix 2

INDEX

Printed in the United States
by Baker & Taylor Publisher Services